THE GERMAN BAROQUE NOVEL

by Hans Wagener

In contrast to traditional histories of the German novel, Professor Wagener describes the three major genres of the German seventeenth-century novel in the sequence of their dominating appearance in Germany: the pastoral, the picaresque, and the courtly-historical novel. He defines the prototype of each genre, either abstractly or by referring to a particular example, discusses the origin of the genre, the influences of foreign models and the modifications by the most prominent German authors of the seventeenth century. Although the study does not deny a historical development and does not exclude biographical sketches of the authors, it does not take an ideo-historical (*geistesgeschichtlich*) or positivistic approach. The emphasis throughout is on the definition of genre criteria and their modification. Interpretations of the individual novels, considering content, style, and structure, are included. Since the authors and the examples chosen are representative of the time and the genres, the study evolves into a presentation of the total spectrum of the German Baroque novel and its genres and authors. It is the first such work which is primarily diachronic in nature.

(TWAS 229)

TWAYNE'S WORLD AUTHORS SERIES (TWAS)

The purpose of TWAS is to survey the major writers —novelists, dramatists, historians, poets, philosophers, and critics—of the nations of the world. Among the national literatures covered are those of Australia, Canada, China, Eastern Europe, France, Germany, Greece, India, Italy, Japan, Latin America, the Netherlands, New Zealand, Poland, Russia, Scandinavia, Spain, and the African nations, as well as Hebrew, Yiddish, and Latin Classical literatures. This survey is complemented by Twayne's United States Authors Series and English Authors Series.

The intent of each volume in these series is to present a critical-analytical study of the works of the writer; to include biographical and historical material that may be necessary for understanding, appreciation, and critical appraisal of the writer; and to present all material in clear, concise English—but not to vitiate the scholarly content of the work by doing so.

The German Baroque Novel

By HANS WAGENER
University of California, Los Angeles

ABOUT THE AUTHOR

Born in Lage/Lippe, Germany, Hans Wagener majored in Germanic studies and history at the universities of Münster/Westf. and Freiburg i. Br., Germany. Since 1964 he has lived in the United States, and he obtained a doctorate in Germanic Languages at the University of California, Los Angeles. Professor Wagener has taught German literature at the University of Southern California and is currently Associate Professor of German at UCLA. In addition to a book on the German Baroque novelist Christian Friedrich Hunold (Menantes), he has co-authored a book on forms of address in the dramas of Andreas Gryphius and published a number of articles on seventeenth century and twentieth century German literature.

York

Preface

Laymen with a serious interest in literature, asked about their knowledge of German Baroque novels, will mention Grimmelshausen's *Simplicissimus*, perhaps several others of Grimmelshausen's novels, and maybe Reuter's *Schelmuffsky*. Even some critics have resigned themselves, in considering the history of the German novel, to start with Goethe's *Wilhelm Meisters Lehrjahre*, possibly including Wieland's *Geschichte des Agathon* as a predecessor. Histories of the German novel often consider Goethe as a starting point. This attitude is understandable: Not only was the German novel (after inconsequential beginnings with Jörg Wickram) virtually a thing of the past around the year 1600, but even one hundred years later the situation had not changed. During the first six decades of the eighteenth century, hardly a work of lasting value—of more than merely literary historical significance—was published, with the exception of Johann Gottfried Schnabel's *Die Insel Felsenburg* (4 vols., 1731/43) and Christian Fürchtegott Gellert's *Die Schwedische Gräfin von G.* (1747/48).

On the other hand, it has become customary to consider as German Baroque literature the lyrical and dramatic style of the seventeenth century, a view originally taken by the German literary historians of the 1920's and 1930's, whose discussion of the term "Baroque" centered around lyrics and drama, and who thereby displayed a total lack of understanding of the monumental works of Lohenstein and Duke Anton Ulrich.

An article written by Arnold Hirsch[1] states that between 1615 and 1669 no more than twenty-nine original novels were published in Germany and fifty-eight translations of foreign novels. Between 1670 and 1724, that is, during the same time span (fifty-four years), three hundred and fifteen original novels and one hundred and fifty-one translations appeared. These statistics indicate, first, the extremely small number of German novels which annually made their appearance on the German book market; and, second, the increase in production of German novels during the last third of the seventeenth and the beginning of the eighteenth centuries, whereas at the same time the relative proportion of translations from foreign languages was decreasing. Quantitative analyses of the catalogues of the great German book fairs in Frankfurt a.M. and Leipzig have proved that during the seventeenth century novels accounted only for a very small percentage of the books published in Germany, since the majority of published works were of a religious nature. Moreover, most of the books at that point were still written in Latin.[2]

Only very slowly novels gained for themselves a place as a recognized poetic genre in Germany. The comments about the novel in the most important treatises on poetics of the seventeenth century can be counted on the fingers of one hand, and in most cases they do not refer to the novel itself but its literary brother, the verse epic,[3] which was venerated by tradition, even though many more novels than epics were written at this time. Novels were considered a corrupting, deceiving influence on the reader's morals. Responsible libraries did not collect them, scholars took no notice of them, scholarly magazines refused to review them, and preachers warned against them;[4] as did, for example, the Zurich moralist Gottard Heidegger in his *Mythoscopia Romantica oder Discours von den so benanten Romans* (Zurich, 1698), who, predicting its imminent downfall, condemns a genre, which, in the meantime, had become extremely popular! It is interesting to note that in all of the characterizations of and polemics against the novel only two of its subgenres are mentioned, namely the pastoral novel and the courtly-historical novel—both of them having been introduced into Germany through translations of famous foreign works—whereas the popular picaresque novel is not even mentioned. A work like Grimmelshausen's *Simplicissimus,* today without a doubt the most widely read German Baroque novel, did not exist for the literary critics and theoreticians of the seventeenth century.

The situation actually has not appreciably changed in the past few decades during a contemporary renaissance of interest in the Baroque period. In general critical treatments and literary histories of German Baroque literature, the novel, with the exception of Grimmelshausen, takes up only a small space in the total work, and the general surveys of the history of the German novel of this period, and the theoretical works on the genre of the novel are small in number. Critical editions of some of the older secondary literature and photomechanical reprints have been in vogue during the past ten years; there also exists quite a body of specialized studies on individual authors, but no general work on the genre itself, no definition of its types formulated by looking at the individual works themselves has made its appearance. Leo Cholevius' work,[5] almost one hundred years old, is valuable mainly due to its detailed plot summaries. Hans Heinrich Borcherdt's *Geschichte des Romans und der Novelle in Deutschland*[6] is too general, due to the fact that its author is primarily interested in the history of ideas, whereas Günther Weydt's history of the German novel up to Goethe's death[7] presents an abundance of material in a well-structured historical sequence, but it is a literary *history* of the novel, not intending to be a description of the genre and its types. Richard Alewyn's essay on the German Baroque novel[8] comes closest to this endeavor, but it is, of course, only a short essay.

Keeping historical development in view, and not excluding biographical sketches of the individual writers, the following presentation, therefore, does not intend to be a history of ideas as manifested in one particular genre, nor an empirically historically oriented *history* of a genre; the main emphasis is rather placed on the description of generic criteria and the variation of the types or subgenres of the novel in the individual works of the most representative authors. The method applied is the following: In dealing with each type of novel the foreign influences are briefly sketched, and, mainly by utilizing a concrete example, the general criteria of the specific genre are defined. Afterward the different variations of the "prototype" are depicted by taking paradigmatic examples from the most important authors. Here, to be sure, general interpretations of the individual works are attempted, including meaning (message), structure, and in some cases, style as well. However, the main emphasis is placed on the question of genre affiliation. It cannot be claimed in all cases that the individual interpretations are original, but the latest available research on the subject is always considered. Since the authors and the selected examples are representative for the period and the genre, the presentation attempts to round out and illustrate the entire spectrum of the German Baroque novel and its types by offering the first primarily diachronic survey of its kind. In the classification into pastoral, picaresque, and courtly-historical novel, I am, to be sure, following the classification suggested by André Jolles[9] and Herbert Singer; however, I distinguish several subgenres as well, stressing the departure from the prototype rather than the features shared with it.

Therefore, in the following study three genres of the seventeenth-century novel with their most important variations will be treated in the sequence of their main appearance in Germany: The *pastoral novel*, being the first to bloom and decline; the *picaresque novel*, which, although introduced into Germany through early translations, did not reach its high point as a German genre before Grimmelshausen and Beer; and the *courtly-historical novel*, since, despite its early exemplary introduction by Opitz in his translation of John Barclay's *Argenis*, most of the great German examples of this genre did not appear before the last third of the seventeenth century.

The Selected Bibliography lists all those works which either deal with the Baroque novel in detail as part of a general treatment or which define and discuss the various subgenres. The most important specialized literature concerning the individual authors or works is given with all bibliographical data in the footnotes. The bibliography also contains a list of all utilized reprints of the German Baroque novels together with the abbreviations used for them in the text, predominantly after direct quotes. The latest critical edition was always used in preference to noncritical older ones. A listing of all editions and translations was not possible for lack of space.

In writing this book, the author is indebted to Professor Eli Sobel, University of California, Los Angeles, and Professor Günther Weydt, University of Münster/Westf., who both stimulated and furthered the author's interest in the German Baroque novel. Many stylistic improvements were suggested by Mrs. Jean Weissenberger.

HANS WAGENER

Contents

Chronology

1559-1595   German translation of the Spanish/French *Amadis* novel (24 vols.).

1614   *Leben vnd Wandel Lazaril von Tormes,* anonymous translation of *La vida de Lazarillo de Tormes* (1554).

1615   Ägidius Albertinus (ca. 1560-1620), *Der Landstörtzer Gusman von Alfarche,* a German adaptation of Mateo Aleman's *Gusman de Alfarache* (1599).

1618   Beginning of the Thirty Years' War.

1624   Martin Opitz (1597-1639), *Buch von der Deutschen Poeterey,* the most influential German Baroque treatise on poetics.

1626   Opitz' translation of John Barclay's *Argenis* (Latin 1621, French 1623).

1630   Opitz, *Schäfferey von der Nimfen Hercinie.*

1632   [anonymous] *Amoena und Amandus.*

1643   Johann Michael Moscherosch (1601-69), *Gesichte Philanders von Sittewald.*

1645   Philipp von Zesen (1619-89), *Die Adriatische Rosemund.*

1648   End of the Thirty Years' War (Peace of Westphalia).

1659-1660   Andreas Heinrich Buchholtz (1607-71), *Herkules und Valiska* (2 vols.).

1663   Johann Thomas (1624-79), *Damon und Lisille.*

1665   Buchholtz, *Herkuliskus und Herkuladisla.*

1667   Hans Jacob Christoffel von Grimmelshausen (ca. 1622-76), *Keuscher Joseph.*

1669   Grimmelshausen, *Der abentheurliche Simplicissimus* and *Continuatio.*

1669-1673   Herzog Anton-Ulrich von Braunschweig-Wolffenbüttel (1633-1714), *Die Durchleuchtige Syrerinn Aramena* (5 vols.).

1670   Grimmelshausen, *Courasche, Der seltzame Springinsfeld, Dietwalt und Amelinde;* Zesen, *Assenat.*

1672   Christian Weise (1642-1708), *Die drei ärgsten Erznarren;* Grimmelshausen, *Proximus und Lympida.*

1672-1673   Grimmelshausen, *Das wunderbarliche Vogelnest,* Parts I and II.

1677-1707   Herzog Anton-Ulrich, *Octavia, Römische Geschichte* (6 vols.).

1680   Johann Beer (1655-1700), *Jucundus Jucundissimus.*

1682   Beer, *Teutsche Winter=Nächte.*

1683   Beer, *Kurtzweilige Sommer=Täge.*

1689   Heinrich Anshelm von Zigler und Kliphausen (1663-96), *Die Asiatische Banise.*

1689-   Daniel Casper von Lohenstein (1635-83), *Arminius und*
1690   *Thusnelda* (2 vols.).

1696   Christian Reuter (ca. 1665-ca. 1712), *Schelmuffsky.*

1702   Christian Friedrich Hunold (Menantes) (1681-1721), *Die liebenswürdige Adalie.*

CHAPTER 1

The Pastoral Novel

I General Genre Criteria and Foreign Influences

THE popularity of the pastoral novel during the seventeenth century can be directly attributed to the sufferings and hardships caused by the Thirty Years' War. Fleeing the misery of their current state, people sought refuge in a world of seemingly simple and natural conditions in which life assumed a dreamlike quality. The pastoral novel is an expression of the desire for a more simple, natural way of life amid the complications of an overrefined culture. Related to this desire is the idealistic concept that virtue is to be found only in nature, that only in nature man can preserve a state of innocence, and that only there liberty, calm, and piety exist. Thus, in the pastoral novel that age-old confrontation between culture and nature—a recurrent theme in world literature and philosophy—is seen.

During the seventeenth century, idealization of the pastoral life became fashionable to an almost ridiculous extreme, and the extent to which people invaded the countryside bordered on the ludicrous. Disguised in shepherd's costumes, they banded together in order to participate in an artificial idyllic country life and sought to free themselves from all conventions. The aristocratic society founded shepherds' clubs, and shepherds' festivals were celebrated. In 1618, for example, the "Akademie der wahren Liebenden" was founded, a princely shepherds' association which counted twenty-nine princes and princesses as well as nineteen other noblemen among its members. These attempts were used to superimpose on real life an artificial and simplified life style which was as internationally accepted and as fashionable as was the literary style of the pastoral novel itself.

What, then is a pastoral novel? It can be defined simply as including all literature that deals with shepherds and their life style, and partly or entirely written in prose. More specifically, the general criteria of the genre are twofold:

13

(1) The shepherd's mask which serves to conceal reality, behind which persons representing reality are disguised, as well as the real life experiences of the poet, his personal circumstances, and his political, religious, or poetic ideas. The pastoral world is a distinctly fictional world, dominated by "pure" love, and often including a mythological touch. Contemporary theoreticians of literature have concluded that pastoral literature represents the original unity of all mankind, a society free from class divisions—the idealized "Golden Age."

(2) The combination of lyric and prose in the same work. Related to this phenomenon is the theory that fiction and reality are blended together in pastoral literature and that such literature is the oldest form of poetic expression.

Before the introduction of the pastoral novel in Germany, the genre could already boast an extensive history in other countries. The first pastoral novel dates back to the time of the Hellenistic period (third century A.D.): Longus' *Daphnis and Chloe*, a novel which, however, had no influence on the consequent development of the genre. The Italian Renaissance displayed a renewed interest in pastoral literature: Boccaccio's *Ninfale d'Ameto* was published in 1341, and in 1502 Jacopo Sannazaro of Naples published his *Arcadia*, the first great pastoral novel of the age. In Spain, Jorge de Montemayor's *Diana*, a novel which was to have a considerable influence on the later German works, appeared in 1541. This work was translated into German by Hans Ludwig von Kuffstein in 1619, together with sequels by Alonzo Perez, Cervantes' *Galatea* (1585), and Lope de Vega's *Arcadia* (1598).

Exerting a similar influence in Germany was Sir Philip Sidney's novel *Arcadia* (written about 1579, published 1590/93). Its first German translation appeared in 1629. A second translation, dating from 1638, was edited and partially rewritten by Martin Opitz, who is considered to be the father of German Baroque literature. Sidney employed the pastoral costume in order to disseminate his own moral and political ideas and to present his own philosophy of life. Thus, the characters in his novel carry on long discussions about such topics as politics, honor, virtue, love and friendship, philosophy, religion, education, and art. The love story as the purveyor of the external action is relegated to the background.

An additional influence on the later German pastoral novels was *Astrée,* a pastoral novel in five volumes by the Frenchman Honoré d'Urfé (1607-27; German 1619 ff.). D'Urfé is credited with having developed a distinctive type of character in his shepherds and shepherdesses, who act in accordance with cavalier modes of behavior. Therefore, the novel was able to become a mirror of gallant, gentlemanlike behavior.

The members of the "Fruchtbringende Gesellschaft"—the most important German *Sprachgesellschaft* (literary society) of the seventeenth century—distinguished themselves by translating the great foreign pastoral novels. These translations then stimulated German writers to create pastoral novels of their own. However, an independent development of this genre in Germany did not begin before the pastoral novel had undergone extensive development in other countries. As a result of the unique sociological, historical, and cultural circumstances in Germany, two distinct forms of the pastoral novel emerged. They can be termed the social pastoral, and the individual-expressive, novel.[1]

II *The Social Pastoral Novel: Martin Opitz'* Schäfferey von der Nimfen Hercinie

In this literary context, "social" is a term indicating a specific group—a courtly society or an association such as a literary society. Social literature of this kind was written for nonartistic purposes; for example, it served to glorify persons of a more elevated social rank or members of some association or society. Thus, the poet restricted himself from the very beginning to a limited reading audience with whom he was well acquainted and who, in turn, were already familiar with his material. The poet needed only to hint at certain things, and the reader, who was familiar with the subject matter, was quite able to fill in the gaps and thereby fully to realize the work. Thus, writer and reader actively cooperated in creating the ultimate effect of the literary work; the extra-artistic reality which the reader was already familiar with served to complete the work of art. In most cases, this limitation of the reading public restricted the number of copies printed. In fact, the knowledge that is necessary in order fully to understand this type of novel renders it almost impossible for the modern reader to relive the reading experiences of the poet's contemporaries. This form of the pastoral novel was always, to a certain extent, a *roman à clef*. To be able to recognize the underlying events and persons behind the pastoral disguise constituted the main enjoyment for its readers. The principal techniques employed for disguise were allegory and the introduction of mythological motifs and characters.

The form of the greater number of social pastoral novels is conversational; the poet himself participates in the dialogue in many cases. Frequently, he himself narrates in the first-person singular. A group of friends, mostly members of the respective social group (disguised as shepherds), discuss the widest variety of topics and partake of common experiences, adventures, and encounters. In addition, this strain of the pastoral novel tended to be a work of two or more poets. This aspect is facilitated by the insertion of lyrical passages, according to the requirements of the genre; indeed, the novel may be reduced to a mere frame for lyrics of the most diverse kind. The Nuremberg poets, members of the literary society called the "Pegnitzschäfer," primarily perfected this form of a common literary enterprise by incorporating into the pastoral novel the dialogue technique as employed by Georg Philipp Harsdörffer (1607-58) in his *Frauenzimmer-Gesprächsspiele* (8 vols., 1641-49). An outstanding example of this kind is the *Pegnesisches Schäfergedicht* (1644-45), a book jointly authored by Harsdörffer, Siegmund von Birken (1626-81) and Johann Klaj (1616-56).

The first independent German pastoral novel, which, on account of its brevity, can only with some hesitation be termed a novel, is Martin Opitz' *Schäfferey von der Nimfen Hercinie* (1630). Opitz was born in Bunzlau/Silesia on December 23, 1597. Following his schooling at the *Gymnasium* in Breslau and Beuthen, he studied law and philosophy at the Universities of Frankfurt a.O. (1618) and Heidelberg (1619), as well as at various localities in Holland. Opitz was constantly on the move, journeying from Jutland to Transylvania, Liegnitz, Breslau, Paris, and Danzig, where he finally fell victim to the plague in 1639 and died. He was a professor at a *Gymnasium*, the secretary of Count Hannibal von Dohna, a diplomat for the dukes of Liegnitz and Brieg, and Polish court historiographer. In 1627 he was knighted as "von Boberfeld," and in 1629 he became a member of the distinguished "Fruchtbringende Gesellschaft." His achievements with regard to the development of the German language and literature are unexcelled; indeed, it was due only to the influence of his *Buch von der Deutschen Poeterey* (1624), a treatise on poetics, which he wrote under the impact of Italian and French Renaissance writings, that an independent German literature was able to emerge in the seventeenth century. Opitz created German models for almost all literary genres, either by translating foreign works or by writing original ones which served as models of German writing.

The main character in the *Schäfferey von der Nimfen Hercinie* is Opitz himself, who narrates in the first person. While taking a walk with some friends in the *Riesengebirge*, they discuss the following topics: loneliness, love, reason, travel, specters, death, and the devil. The companions meet the nymph Hercinie, who shows them through magnificent subterranean grottos (a motif that has been borrowed from Sannazaro's *Arcadia*) and who, in addition, praises the achievements of the Schaffgotsch family, a family of Silesian nobility. The praise of Count Schaffgotsch, to whom the novelette is dedicated, constitutes its high point. Toward the end, the friends witness an example of the uses of witchcraft to obtain love.

Opitz' friends appear under their real names (Nüßler, Buchner), and are also costumed as shepherds. The world of the novel is a typical mixture of nymphs and shepherds, mixing the reality of the present with the mythological past. The presence of Opitz and his friends as well as the glorification of the Schaffgotsch family makes the work a piece of social literature—Opitz was at that time living as a guest on the family estate. The characteristic of pastoral poetry, that is, of creating a world opposed to reality, was suited to Opitz' intentions; he depicts an idyll in the *Riesengebirge* which he deliberately contrasts with the rage and destruction of the Thirty Years' War.

However, the significance of the novel does not become clear merely from summarizing its content and indicating the fulfillment of the genre requirements. The problem the poet is confronted with at the beginning is that of deciding whether to remain at home with a girl he loves or whether to undertake a planned trip to Paris. The decision he finally arrives at after lengthy discussions with his friends is that, whereas sensual love is bound to external beauty, spiritual love is free from time and place. Therefore, it is possible for him to take the trip; indeed, it is even desirable to do so, especially if it is undertaken in the service of the homeland. The examples set by the house of Schaffgotsch demonstrate that leaving home and country in the service of the fatherland is desirable, whereas the fairy tale about the nymph stresses the fact that home is the ideal place to be. The witchcraft episode with its love spell proves to the poet that his own love is not altogether sensual; therefore, he can travel abroad with a good conscience and still remain faithful to his beloved. The conflict between love for one's native country and the urge to experience the distant unknown is combined with the worldly glorification of the Schaffgotsch family and with a description of nature, which the poet draws from firsthand experience.[2]

It has already been stated that the dialogue form of the *Schäfferey* was taken over by the Nuremberg poets. As in so many of his other works, Opitz' *Schäfferey* set an example which opened the way for an entire series of German pastoral novels. In addition to Opitz' work and the *Pegnesisches Schäfergedicht,* the following works must be mentioned as further examples of the social pastoral novel: Paul Fleming, *Brockmans Hochzeit* (1635), Philipp von Zesen, *Rosenwälder Vorschmack* (1642), and a number of novels by Siegmund von Birken, such as *Norischer Parnaß* and *Norischer Phöbus* (both 1677), which show signs of a more realistic style.[3]

III   *The Individual-Expressive Pastoral Novel:* Amoena und Amandus *and Johann Thomas'* Damon und Lisille

This type of pastoral novel does not deal with any specific society or group, nor does it glorify any particular persons or noble families; rather, the poet writes from his own personal need, from an inner desire to express his own emotional or spiritual experience—in most cases a particular love experience. This type of pastoral novel is, therefore, autobiographical, although the author attempts to conceal his identity behind a pseudonym and gives the main character a noncommital name. Personal experience—indeed, the poet's *own* experience—is the essence of this genre. A vividly descriptive style is consequently one of its hallmarks.

From this basic difference between the two types of pastoral novel the following conclusions can be drawn: In contrast to the social pastoral novel, the individual-expressive novel is self-sufficient, insofar as the novel is not addressed to a particular group and, therefore, does not presuppose a knowledge about the group in order to be understood by the reader. Instead, the reader experiences it by focusing inward and by reliving the author's personal experience. The pastoral elements receive less attention; at times, the characters are termed shepherds but do not display any shepherd characteristics. This demonstrates that individual-expressive literature is a contradiction of the typifying, idealizing pastoral disguise.

Because of its autobiographical character, the novel is not as abstractly constructed as its socially oriented counterpart. Whereas in the social pastoral novel the inserted lyrical passages are often easily interchangeable, the "novel" itself being only a backdrop or a narrative frame for the author's or authors' lyrics, the lyrics in the individual-expressive pastoral novel are directly related and are thus essential to the content. They are either indispensable to the expression of the poet's or the characters' emotions, or they promote the action. Because of the autobiographical character, this type of novel is, in most cases, open ended: The fate of the lovers is not yet decided, or it has been decided against their wishes; and a separation is proved inevitable.[4] Thus, it is evident that the two types of pastoral novel are quite different (except for the external criteria of the genre itself as explained at the beginning of this chapter).

The first actual pastoral novel in Germany and, at the same time, one of the best examples of the individual-expressive type was published two years after Opitz' *Schäfferey.* Its full title is: *Jünst=erbawete Schäfferey, Oder Keusche Liebes=Beschreibung, Von der Verliebten Nimfen AMOENA, Vnd dem Lobwürdigen Schäffer AMANDUS* [. . .] Durch A. S. D. D. Leipzig, [. . .] 1632. The author is unknown; however, it is very probable that the experiences he reports are indeed his own. The decoding of the anagram of the hero's name makes this the more likely and provides clues as to how the author's identity may be established. The main character calls himself Amandus von Walechim aus Elisien. Walechim in Elisia, however, is Michelau in Silesia, a small locality in the vicinity of Brieg which, at that time, belonged to the bachelor Baron Hans Adam von Gruttschreiber und Czopkendorff. Although the author's identity is not certain, the story takes place, in any case, among the gentry living between Michelau and a small town on the Oder River. This short novel was an unparalleled success. By 1665 it had had twelve printings and was widely imitated.

The plot is a very simple one: Amoena, whose father is "a prince and leader of all [...] shepherds," falls in love with Amandus, who is also highborn. He returns her love, but only for a while; not only has he been persuaded against loving her by a friend, but the same advice is dictated by the voice of his own reason, which makes him doubt that his love for Amoena is real and that Amoena is in fact as beautiful as he had imagined. He abandons his beloved to take a journey which he had already planned to take previous to their meeting.

All the external requirements of the genre of the pastoral novel are met. The work is a mixture of poetry and prose; there are mythological dreams as well as a description of a painting of Pyramus and Thisbe (frequently encountered in pastoral novels as a model of an ill-fated love match); and as the initial challenging problem the question as to whether the shy Amoena should fall victim to love or not arises. The pastoral elements appear only in a very superficial form, however: The chief of the shepherds lives in a city, and the "hero" of the novel once attends to his flock; but it is obvious that here a writer who wants to describe his own experiences uses the shepherd's disguise and that the playful atmosphere is secondary to the problem being dealt with.

As stated in the foreword, the novel attempts to provide guidance in resolving a conflict of conscience in an exemplary manner, recommending moderation in love (*AA*, p. 9). Important in this respect is the discrepancy between the logical argumentation of the friend and the hero's own reasoning, which finally leads to the actual solution. The friend reasons with him, using the popular arguments of contemporary ethics: He condemns the hero's love of Amoena because it is not sanctioned by marriage; such a passion must be sinful because it does not give man any true and lasting spiritual happiness (*AA*, pp. 76 ff.). The novel probably owes its success to the fact that this ethical judgment is in agreement with the ruling moral code of the time.[5]

The decision is made because of the above-mentioned journey, which Amandus wishes to undertake in order to further his education and increase his fortune, a problem somewhat similar to the one treated in Opitz' *Schäfferey von der Nimfen Hercinie.* The ultimate goal of his journey, however, is neither service to the home country nor moral integrity but rather temporal, material values. Thus, these values take on an importance which they could never attain in a courtly-historical novel.

Literary critics have accorded the highest praise to the pastoral novel, *Damon und Lisille.* Heinrich Meyer, for example, terms it genuinely great literature, and, with the exception of Grimmelshausen's *Simplicissimus,* perhaps "the most beautiful novel of the seventeenth century."[6] Paul Hankamer praises the unique magic of the tender, passionate, and joyous affection of the two lovers for each other; he praises the sweet sensual charm, the tender, affectionate description of all of the human as well as natural surroundings which are so irradiated by the joy of love that the golden aura of the idyll is carried far and above the objective, concrete framework of the novel. Hankamer terms the book a "unique miracle."[7]

The anagrammatic pseudonyms of the author, Matthias Jonsohn and J. Mostain, conceal his true identity; he was Johann Thomas, a court official of the duke of Saxony-Altenburg. Thomas had one of the most amazing careers possible for a commoner during the seventeenth century. Born in 1624, he became full professor of law at the University of Jena at the age of twenty-six. In 1653 he was made ambassador at the Diet of Regensburg; in 1658, ducal representative at the election of the new emperor in Frankfurt a.M.; and, after numerous other diplomatic missions, was eventually made consistorial president, privy councilor, and finally chancellor of the duchy. He died in 1679. His only literary work is dedicated to his wife, Elisabeth (Lisille), who died in childbed after two years of marriage. The novel has appeared in at least three editions.[8]

The novel treats, in pastoral disguise, the love, courtship, engagement, wedding, and marriage of Damon and Lisille. The narrative is related in the third person; lyrics and prose alternate. It appears to be at first glance a typical pastoral novel. What, then, is so special about it? In what way is it elevated above other examples of the genre? Primarily, its value resides in the simple and unpretentious, but genuinely felt, cordial, and graceful style, prevailing in the prose sections as well as in the lyrical ones. Because of its lack of preciosity and bucolic over-sweetness this style creates an atmosphere unusual for the seventeenth century. It is the warmth combined with subtlety and discreetness which are responsible for the transformation of genuinely experienced feelings into poetical language. The culmination of this new style is the description of the wedding and wedding night (*DL*, pp. 31 ff.).

Novel also to *Damon und Lisille* is the theme. In contemporary courtly-historical novels it was very customary to treat as themes love, courtship, engagement, and wedding; however, the wedding usually took place at the end of the novel and not at midpoint. During the seventeenth century, marriage itself was not considered a worthy topic for writing about—it was no literary subject. From Book V on—the novel is subdivided into twelve books—Thomas describes "wie doch diese Ehe geraten" ("how this marriage turned out to be"). He tells how Damon and Lisille had to shoulder good and bad times, which they were able to bear because they rendered each other mutual aid (*DL*, p. 39). He tells of financial troubles, outings into the countryside, farewells and homecomings, the sickness and death of a child, good and evil neighbors, and so forth. The interspersed lyrics deal with anything from the vanity of human life to the sanitary insufficiencies of the inns; they span a range of subjects extending from the loftiest to the most trivial.

Thomas' pastoral novel does not merely deal with love, the beauty of a girl, and her wedding to a handsome shepherd, in a lighthearted, flirtatious manner; rather, it deals with the trials this love encounters in everyday life and with the difficulties of marriage as well as with its idealized joys.

To be sure, Thomas does use literary commonplaces and themes which were popular during the Baroque period, as, for example, the recognition of the transitory nature of time. The conscience of the transience of all earthly things, however, is transformed by this diplomat and man of the world into a moderate *carpe diem* at the conclusion:

> Doch ist bey dieser Flüchtigkeit
> Noch ein gewinn der Zeit /
> Sich lieben vnd küssen /

Das Hertz vnd Gewissen
Nicht schmählern noch kräncken /
Vnd immer gedencken /
Wie flüchtig sey die Zeit. (*DL*, p. 106)

Yet in spite of this transitoriness
Time allows one gain
To love and to kiss
Which is not impaired nor offended
By heart and conscience
Nor by the continual awareness
Of the transitory nature of time.

In this way, Thomas places his own experience and his own subjective feeling above the recognized standards of his time. He proves to be far ahead of his great poetic contemporaries.[9] Thomas places his individual consciousness of his love for Lisille above the vanity of all earthly things:

Noch eins / das ist der Zeit
in meinem Leben
Der schnöden Eytelkeit
nicht vntergeben /
Verachtet für und für
Fortunen willen /
Die Liebe zwischen mir
vnd der Lisillen. (*DL*, p. 62)

One additional thing
which is not controlled
By time, by vile vanity
in my life
Which deeply despises
Fortune's wishes
That is the love between me
and Lisille.

A more pronounced example of the individual-expressive pastoral novel than is given in these lines is simply inconceivable.

During the four decades after the publication of *Amoena und Amandus*, the individual-expressive pastoral novel flourished. In addition to Zesen's *Die Adriatische Rosemund* and Thomas' *Damon und Lisille* the following novels deserve to be mentioned: *Coelinde und Corymbo* (1636), *Die verwüstete und verödete*

Schäferey (1642), both anonymous; Jakob Schweiger's *Die verführte Schäferin Cynthie* (1660), [anonymous] *Zweyer Schäfer Neu gepflanzter Liebesgarten* (1661), Johann Joseff Bekkh's *Elbianische Florabella* (1667), and [anonymous] *Thorheit der Verliebten* (1668). None of these novels, with the exception of *Damon und Lisille,* contains a happy ending.

By the end of the seventeenth century the pastoral novel, which showed realistic and satirical tendencies in its later offshoots, was no longer utilized as a literary form. Pastoral motifs, however, lived on, not only in the later forms of the courtly-historical novel, but in the Rococo poetry of the eighteenth century as well. Historically, it is significant that the pastoral novel in its autobiographical form anticipated the individualistic novel of the eighteenth century, which, as a result of the individualistic, soul-searching energies of Pietism, then made its appearance.

IV *Philipp von Zesen*: Die Adriatische Rosemund

Philipp von Zesen's novel *Die Adriatische Rosemund* has been acclaimed by recent critics not only as the first German *Kunstroman* but also as an autobiographical novel having an artist as its main character, as well as being the first and only representative *Liebesroman* (romance) of German seventeenth-century literature.[10] Because of these three classifications, its treatment here as a pastoral novel must be clarified.

Philipp von Zesen was born on October 8, 1619, in Priorau, a village in the vicinity of Dessau/Saxony. He attended high school in Halle and studied at the Universities of Wittenberg and Leipzig, where he apparently graduated in 1642 with an M. A. degree. Much of his life he spent traveling and moving back and forth between Holland and Hamburg. His travels also took him to England and France. His extensive correspondence points to social contacts with high-ranking acquaintances and friends. In 1643 in Hamburg he founded the *Deutschgesinnte Genossenschaft,* also called *Rosengesellschaft,* a literary society which was patterned after the *Fruchtbringende Gesellschaft,* the goal of which was to promote the German language as well as to cultivate the friendship of its members. Zesen retained the chairmanship of the society under the sobriquet "der Fertige" until his death. His society included among its membership such celebrities as the Dutch dramatist Jost van den Vondel (1587-1679) and the German satirist and translator Hans Michael Moscherosch (1601-69). In 1653 Zesen was granted nobility by Emperor Ferdinand III at the Diet of Regensburg. As an imperial *Hofpfalzgraf* (Count Palatine) he himself later granted poets the laurel crown and derived an income from it, as did Andreas Gryphius' patron Schönborn. At the age of fifty-two, Zesen married a nineteen-year-old girl; the marriage, however, was childless. He died in Hamburg on November 13, 1689.

Zesen's life was extraordinarily interesting due to the fact that his relatively long life spans the period of the Thirty Years' War as well as that of the political reorganization of Germany after the Peace of Westphalia in 1648. This time span must be regarded as embracing two socially and culturally different periods. In addition, Zesen's life style differed radically from that of other German poets of the seventeenth century in that he did not enter the service of a prince, as did Opitz, nor hold any high-ranking administrative or diplomatic position, as did Andreas Gryphius or Daniel Casper von Lohenstein. Zesen can be considered as the first German free-lance writer; he was a man who made the attempt to earn a living simply by writing and translating and to conduct his life as an independent man of letters. The most famous Dutch publishing companies employed him as an editor, reader, and translator. His own translations and writings were his main profession, however, and were not the product of his leisure, as was the case with other writers of his time. A work on poetics (*Hochdeutscher Helikon*, 1640), is attributed to Zesen as well as are several collections of poems, and he is also credited with the translation of several novels. During the year in which his original novel *Die Adriatische Rosemund* came out, there also appeared *Ibrahim* [...] *und der Beständigen Isabellen Wunder-Geschichte* (1645), a translation of Mlle de Scudéry's *Ibrahim*. Two years later (1647) he published *Die Afrikanische Sophonisbe,* a translation of the French novel by Sieur de Gerzan of the same title. Of the poet's two religious novels, *Assenat* (1670) and *Simson* (1679), the former will subsequently be analyzed.

The plot of *Die Adriatische Rosemund* can be summarized briefly. At the home of friends in Holland, the young German

Markhold makes the acquaintance of the beautiful Rosemund from Venice. A proposal of marriage follows. Since, however, Markhold is a Protestant and Rosemund's family is Catholic, her father consents to the marriage only under the condition that Rosemund remain Catholic and that any daughters are to be raised in the Catholic faith. Markhold agrees only that Rosemund be allowed to retain her religious beliefs; but insists that his children, on the other hand, be educated as Protestants. Due to this tragic difference of opinion, the two lovers cannot be united. Moreover, not only does Rosemund temporarily withdraw into a pastoral existence, as she begins to doubt Markhold's faithfulness, but in her despair over the situation regarding their union, she contracts a fatal illness and slowly wastes away. The outcome is left for the reader to guess: Rosemund's death is not mentioned, but there is obviously no hope for a happy outcome.

As may be evident from this summary, the novel is distinguished by a dearth of action as well as by a definite lack of activity on the part of the characters. This peculiarity can be accounted for by the fact that the work has affinities with different types of the novel, as we hope to be able to demonstrate.

Die Adriatische Rosemund is a *roman à clef,* although the modern reader cannot identify most of the characters. Zesen's stylization of his characters is to a great extent responsible for this failure. Max Jellinek, for example, has attempted to identify Rosemund's family in the archives of Venice, naturally without success (comp. *AR,* p. XLVI). It is just as naïve to seek the real Rosemund in a laundry in Leipzig (Zesen is rumored to have been enamored of a girl working in such an establishment while he was a student in Leipzig). We may well assume that Rosemund was patterned after a real person, but because of Zesen's stylization of her we cannot identify her as a specific historical figure. From approximately twelve main characters and five supporting ones it has been possible thus far to identify two:

(1) In Paris Markhold has a friend, a certain Wahrmund von der Tannen, which was the sobriquet of the poet Jesaias Rompler von Löwenhalt, the founder of the *Aufrichtige Tannengesellschaft,* which was one of the most influential literary societies of the seventeenth century.

(2) Markhold himself is the poet Philipp von Zesen, since "Mark-hold" is simply a literal translation into German of the Greek "Philipp" ("fond of horses").[11] Another clue to his identity is the dominance of the color blue. Not only does Zesen, as the author, refer to himself by the pseudonym "Ritterhold von Blauen," but in the novel as well the color blue constitutes a sort of leitmotiv. Rosemund's shepherd's cottage is furnished with blue carpets; the floor is covered with blue tile; the ceiling is painted blue; and a painting in the room depicts a knight in blue armor (*AR*, pp. 96 f.). The connection with the author's pseudonym is obvious, apart from the fact that the latinized form of Zesen = "caesius" also is translated as "blue-gray." This parallel, however, is not restricted to the name alone, for Zesen's and Markhold's lives during the time of the novel's action are identical, so that we may assume that *Die Adriatische Rosemund* is an autobiographical novel to some extent.

If, on the one hand, biographical facts of Zesen's life may be utilized to shed light on the events depicted in the novel, the novel itself, on the other hand, may serve to clarify biographical facts of Zesen's life in 1643 and 1644. The exact dates may have been altered slightly in the novel in order to compress the main plot into the time span of exactly one year, as was stipulated in the theoretical foreword of Mlle de Scudéry's *Ibrahim*,[12] which Zesen translated. This limitation makes it necessary, for example, for the novel to commence in the middle of the action and for the previous events pertinent to the story to be subsequently reported, an *in medias res* technique which will be found again in the courtly-historical novel. Accordingly, Zesen begins the main plot of the novel in July, 1643; he himself traveled to Paris in May of the same year. Although the requirements of the genre have forced the author to make small adjustments, that is, "corrections" of reality as pertains to date and time of events, these changes have not impaired the novel's autobiographical content.

The climax of the novel is Rosemund's flight into a shepherdess's life. The heroine becomes a shepherdess because doing so, above all, entails a retreat from the world—but not an ultimate one, as, for example, would be the case if she had taken a vow or entered a monastery. The symbolic-ideal character of this period of retreat becomes especially clear in the above-mentioned description of the shepherd's cottage, which becomes a temple to Rosemund's glorification of Markhold and, therefore, an indirectly symbolic expression of Zesen's self-glorification. Thus, Rosemund's life as a shepherdess is not only a disappointed girl's retreat from the world but also the retreat to an ideal atmosphere, an ideal for the complete idealization of a love which is not possible in the "actual reality." It is the creation of a world which is appropriate to the "celestial Rosemund."

Pastoral motifs can be found in other parts of the novel as well; for example, the singing and piping of the shepherds and shepherdesses on the banks of the Amstel River (*AR*, p. 63), or, in the independent tale of Guht=muht, which has been inserted by the author. Guht=muht is asked by an old shepherd to select the most beautiful from three young women—an obvious variant of the Paris legend (*AR*, pp. 119 ff.). Also taken from the pastoral novel is the recurrent motif of affixing poems to trees, so that they will be found by the beloved, as Markhold does, for example, at the beginning of Book V. Indeed, all of the lyrical passages at various places throughout the novel, where Markhold praises Rosemund, and all of the correspondence between the lovers, written in the forms of poems, are elements of the pastoral novel. These, however, are not the only lyrics the novel contains: Following the "end" of the novel, there is an additional anthology of Zesen's poems, most of them addressed to Rosemund. These poems definitely must be viewed as part of the novel. They reinforce the characteristic form of the novel as a vehicle for the author's lyrics—a characteristic that takes the work further into the sphere of the pastoral novel. Emphasis on the lyric element, on the creation of an idyllic atmosphere rather than on plot development, accounts for a lack of action, which is one of the criteria for the pastoral novel. As a means of symbolic representation of love or as a vehicle for the introduction of popular mythological characters and stories, the pastoral novel frequently contains descriptions of paintings; "Pyramus and Thisbe," for example, was a subject which was particularly popular. As in the individual-expressive pastoral novels, the love story of the main characters is autobiographical, and the lovers are not united by marriage at the end. The novel ends in a hopelessness which is the equivalent to separation. The presence of all these criteria allows us to conclude that

Zesen's *Die Adriatische Rosemund* may be considered primarily a pastoral novel despite the presence of features characteristic of other types of novels.

The unhappy end distinguishes *Die Adriatische Rosemund* decisively from the courtly-historical novel.[13] A principle, however, which *Die Adriatische Rosemund* has in common with the courtly-historical novels of the time is the above-mentioned *in medias res* technique—the filling-in of the action which has taken place previous to the onset of the novel, this being a principle which the courtly-historical novel had taken over from Heliodor's late Greek novel.[14] In comparison with *Die Adriatische Rosemund*, the German and French courtly-historical novels of the seventeenth century are much more voluminous, however; they interweave a greater number of individual plots, and the fates of large numbers of couples with their respective marriages result in the apotheosis of a happy end. *Die Adriatische Rosemund*, by comparison, is restricted to one couple and is consequently a comparatively short novel. In addition, Zesen's work has a much looser structure than the usual courtly-historical novel. It is thus evident that *Die Adriatische Rosemund* combines the European traditions of the individual-expressive pastoral novel and the stylized courtly-historical novel.

Die Adriatische Rosemund contains various kinds of inserted elements: poetry, correspondence, descriptions of paintings, novellas, and scholarly essays. Although it has already been shown that the lyrical insertions meet the requirements of the pastoral novel, their function in such a complex work as *Die Adriatische Rosemund* has not yet been accounted for. In addition to fulfilling requirements of the genre, the lyrics offered the twenty-five-year-old Zesen the chance to express feelings and sensations in a concentrated form,[15] poetry being the purest means of expressing emotions. The letters interspersed throughout the novel have a similar function since through these feelings can also be allowed to surface. *Die Adriatische Rosemund* contains five letters which are rendered verbatim, three of them exchanged by Markhold and Rosemund. These are not merely expressions of the persons' feelings, they also stimulate feelings in others and promote the action of the story. When Markhold, for example, sends a report about his first trip to France, the letter triggers feelings of distrust, suspicion, and unrequited love—sensations which eventually compel Rosemund to seek the life of a shepherdess. The letters in *Die Adriatische Rosemund* are not merely stylistic exercises and model examples of Zesen's letter style but fulfill a very concrete function.

The novel contains two scholarly treatises, which mutually complement each other: Rosemund and her father Sünnebald offer a detailed description of Venice and its political Constitution; and Markhold counters with a history and description of the German peoples (*AR*, pp. 154 ff. and pp. 192 ff.). From an esthetic point of view both essays are unrelated to the novel. Their style is extremely dry, since their content is restricted to a mere enumeration of scholarly facts, which do not seem at all suited to the speech of Rosemund. Zesen has drawn them from numerous sources, among others from Merian's *Archontologia Cosmica*. The sources are clearly listed in the poet's footnotes, although he occasionally displays his somewhat superficial manner in the obvious misunderstanding of his sources. Yet the essays cannot be simply ignored by concluding that they have no relation to the problems of the novel;[16] but they must be viewed in light of the seventeenth-century poet's own conception: The seventeenth-century poet is a poet as well as scholar and desires to show himself in both capacities. The poetical theories of the age justify the insertion of scholarly essays. It was an age which stressed variety as an important criterion of the work of art. The treatises on poetics ascribed variety to the epic, and it was, consequently, applied to the novel as its close relative. To what extent Zesen's example set a precedent will be seen by examining the courtly-historical novels, most of which appeared in the second half of the seventeenth century.

Apart from these scholarly essays, *Die Adriatische Rosemund* contains several interpolated novellas, namely, love stories, which are narrated by the main characters of the novel. "Der Lust=wandel des Guhts=muhts" (*AR*, pp. 119 ff.) narrates the encounter of a poor student with a number of beautiful girls, using the Paris motif; "Di Begäbnüs Der Böhmischen Gräfin und des Wild=fangs" (*AR*, pp. 129 ff.) demonstrates how a lover, by means of scheming and intrigue, supplants his rival, who was previously favored by the lady. More interesting because of its closer relation to the main action of the novel is the third novella, which Markhold relates to the ailing Rosemund on the occasion of his last visit; it is entitled "Eine Nider=ländische geschicht von einer ahdlichen Jungfrauen und einem Rit=meister." A maiden falls in love with a captain. However, her parents want her to marry another, older and richer, suitor. But she allows herself to be seduced by the captain and then marries him. Her parents, who promptly disinherit her, are reconciled with her after her first baby is born. The parallel of the situation in the story to the circumstances described in the novel cannot be overlooked. However, the motivation is not the same: In both cases the father withholds his approval of his daughter's marriage; but whereas he does so out of pure avarice in the "Nider=ländische geschicht," in the main plot of *Die Adriatische Rosemund* he does so because of the difference of religion. In the "Nider=ländische geschicht" the obstacle is a purely worldly one, having its roots in a weakness of character. It allows active resistance and therefore can be overcome. In the main plot of *Die Adriatische Rosemund* the difference in religion presents itself to Markhold as an insurmountable obstacle, as fate.[17] Markhold is not antagonistic to Rosemund's father. Because of this motivational and circumstantial difference it would not seem to be justified to view the "Nider=ländische geschicht" as a suggested positive outcome of the unfinished Rosemund-Markhold-plot.[18] On the contrary, whereas in the one case a marriage is possible, in the other case such a solution is impossible because of the difference of circumstances.

If one views the two heroes, Markhold and the captain, in relation to their respective lovers, another differentiating characteristic, which places the genre-affiliation of *Die Adriatische Rosemund* in a new light, becomes obvious. For, whereas the captain is prepared to fight for his love without hesitation, Markhold's "love" is of a totally different nature. As early as in the "foreplot," in which Markhold explains to his friend what has taken place before the novel actually begins, he confessses that he had been attracted to Rosemund more out of "mit=leiden" (compassion) than from actual desire; he had viewed her more with fascination and a sort of holy fear than with actual love, considering her too elevated for his love (*AR*, pp. 45 f.). In other words: Markhold does not actually love Rosemund in the ordinary sense of the word; he merely venerates her and has compassion for her, and no more. Whereas

Rosemund could obviously defy even her own father's will, Markhold resigns himself to accepting the father's verdict as his fate. Over and over again he leaves Rosemund and undertakes journeys which have no respectable or noteworthy motivation, and from which he writes restrained letters and poems. His poems, however, are not only addressed to Rosemund but also to the beautiful Heldinne in Paris. Markhold's love flourishes in Rosemund's absence, rather than in her presence, which poses a threat to him, as he is first and foremost a poet, not a lover. In fact, Zesen has created an autobiographical novel which deals with the specific attitude of a poet toward life, thus constituting the first *Künstlerroman* in German literature.[19]

The action of the novel does, in fact, take place at the time of the Thirty Years' War, but in contrast to Grimmelshausen's *Simplicissimus*, for example, the reality of the war does not permeate it. As was the case with so many seventeenth-century poets, Zesen spent those years in the Netherlands, where the effects of the war were unfelt. On the contrary, the Netherlands had a flourishing and peaceful bourgeois culture. It was this very culture together with the à la mode culture of Paris, which provided the background of the novel, supplying the framework upon which Markhold's character is built. Markhold is no picaresque Simplicius, who is driven from place to place by the events of the war, but his life mirrors the bourgeois existence of his author, who realized his ideals by living as a free-lance writer. Urbanity and the social qualities of the hero are brought to the forefront and elevated during his stay in Paris. Markhold does not belong to the high nobility, as do the heroes of the courtly-historical novels, but is rather a representative of the patrician class culture, depicted here as Zesen had experienced it in Amsterdam. *Die Adriatische Rosemund* is thus one of the earliest examples of a novel reflecting the bourgeois culture in the German literature of the seventeenth century.[20]

In *Die Adriatische Rosemund*, Zesen intended to glorify himself as an independent bourgeois poet. This is most evident in the stylization of Rosemund herself. There are various indications which suggest that Rosemund actually lived; previously, in 1644, Zesen had dedicated his translation of *Lysander und Kaliste* to the "überirdische Rosemund" ("the celestial Rosemund"), and he also mentions her in the preface of his *Ibrahim* translation. However, Rosemund extends beyond being a mere portrait; it is no accident, for example, that Zesen makes May 1 Rosemund's birthday. That date is Zesen's own name day, as well as the date on which he founded his *Deutschgesinnte Genossenschaft*. Thus, it can scarcely be denied that a connection can be seen between his literary society with its *Rosenzunft* ("guild of the rose") and Rosemund.[21] The guild of the rose, the head of which was Zesen himself, stood for the ideal of Zesen's love and adoration, just as Markhold had adored Rosemund. Markhold's letter seal, which is reproduced on the etching which appears on the title page, depicts two hearts chained together. A palm tree is growing from one of the hearts, a rose from the other. Next to it is written the sentence "Last hägt Lust" ("sorrow breeds happiness"). Zesen himself had as a guild symbol the "Indic palm tree," with a "wreath of roses." The motto of his guild was also "Last häget Lust," the motto with which Markhold and Rosemund used to signify their eternal faithfulness (*AR*, p. 20). Thus, Rosemund proves to be a symbol of faithfulness in Zesen's *Deutschgesinnte Genossenschaft*. This indicates that Zesen did not write his novel for a large anonymous reading public, but rather for the relatively small group of friends in the *Deutschgesinnte Genossenschaft*. Probably no more than a few hundred copies of the novel were printed.

In *Die Adriatische Rosemund,* Zesen uses a vocabulary and an orthography which is strikingly different from those used by other German poets of the seventeenth century.[22] He was not only a poet but also a reformer of the German language, and he created *Die Adriatische Rosemund* according to a unique set of orthographical rules which he himself postulated, and which he had already promulgated two years earlier in his *Hoch-Deutsche=Spraachübung*. His new orthography followed two basic principles: a phonetically correct representation of the words (phonographic principle) and an indication of the etymology of the words (etymological principle). If the words are pronounced according to Zesen's spelling, it is immediately obvious that the basis for his orthography is the upper Saxon or Misnian dialect, which had canonical authority with regard to pronunciation among the educated classes from the middle of the sixteenth until the second half of the eighteenth century.

Zesen's suggestions and rules were not accepted by the wider reading public, however, so that he later abandoned his radical standpoint. The traditional spelling of the German language could not be supplanted by an orthography that was based on the pronunciation of a spoken dialect of one single region.

The appendix to the novel contains a brief index of the most prominent new words which Zesen himself had coined (*AR*, pp. 269 f.). There are some well-known examples, such as "pistohl, reit=puffer," "fänster, tage=leuchter," "nonnen=kloster; Jungfer=zwünger" and so on, examples which have since been ridiculed again and again. However, not all new words which Zesen coined gave as amusing an impression as these examples. A considerable number of them have been permanently established as part of the present-day German vocabulary: "Befehlshaber" for "Commandant," "Handlung" for "Actus," "Sinnbild" for "Symbolum," "Staatsmann" for "Politicus," or "bequem" for "capabel." Zesen's endeavors to substitute German words for loan words, that is, for words of foreign origin, must be viewed in light of the struggle of the German poets against a cultural suppression of the Germanic by the Romance culture—a tendency against which German poets struggled until the second half of the seventeenth century.[23]

To summarize: In Zesen's *Die Adriatische Rosemund* elements of various genres of the novel have been incorporated: the pastoral novel, the courtly-historical novel, and the autobiographical *Künstlerroman*. Zesen's novel has proved to be a unique one, as it is the first attempt of an author to describe personal experiences in a novel without considerably altering the actual circumstances.[24] In addition, it has been shown to be the true memorial of Zesen's love for his circle of friends in the *Deutschgesinnte Genossenschaft,* an effect which he was able to achieve by symbolically stylizing Rosemund. The novel displays Zesen's bourgeois attitude toward life and thereby anticipates a development of the German novel, which was not to gain a new impetus until the middle of the eighteenth century with the establishment of the German bourgeois *Kunstroman.* Its importance to literary history can thus clearly be seen.

CHAPTER 2

The Picaresque Novel

I *Foreign Influences and Genre Criteria*: Leben vnd Wandel
Lazaril von Tormes

THE picaresque novel is a type which originated in six-teenth-century Spain. Since many Spanish picaresque novels were soon translated into German, either literally or in a revised and edited form, they are of special interest here.

The first Spanish picaresque novel, *La vida de Lazarillo de Tormes*, was published anonymously in Burgos in 1554. Two additional printings followed in the same year, and during the following decades, numerous editions were published in Spain, Italy, and also in the Netherlands.[1] The author of this novel is still unknown. The book was soon relegated to the Papal Index and appeared in suitably abridged editions, sometimes with sequels. The first German translation, which was not published until very recently, dates from 1614 (*=LT*). The first printed translation by Niklas Ulenhart was published in 1617 in Augsburg. Attached was another picaresque novel, *Die History von Isaak Winckelfelder vnd Jobst von der Schneid,* a reworked version of Cervantes' novella *Rinconete y Cortadillo* (1613). Whereas Cervantes describes the life and activities of the gang of thieves of Seville, Ulenhart made Prague the locale for the action, skillfully adapting the conditions peculiar to Spain to those of Bohemia. By the middle of the eighteenth century, both translations had been reprinted several times, separately and jointly.

In 1615, that is, two years before, the German translation of another Spanish picaresque novel was published: Mateo Alemán's *Gusman de Alfarache.* Published for the first time in 1599—almost half a century after *Lazarillo* (which set the standards for the genre)—*Gusman* was reprinted twenty-five times within six years. This was an unparalleled success. The German translator was the Bavarian court secretary and librarian, Ägidius Albertinus (1560-1620), who, as a result of his rendition, later became known as the "father of the German picaresque novel." He was already well known as the author and translator of numerous moralistic and edifying works. Actually, only the first part of his translation is an edited version of the Spanish original, whereas the second part is an entirely new work by Albertinus, a moralistic and dogmatic-ascetic treatise concerning repentance and remorse. The third part, the pseudonymous author of which calls himself Martinus Freudenhold, describes Gusman's pilgrimage to Jerusalem, his adventures among pirates, and his eventual return. It was Albertinus' *Gusman* translation which later had considerable influence on Grimmelshausen's *Simplicissimus*. It became so popular that it was published in Munich in 1616, 1617, 1618, and 1631.

Just as, subsequently, there appeared a female counterpart to Defoe's *Robinson Crusoe*, there was also a female *picara*. In 1620 *Die Landstörtzerin Justina Dietzin,* based on an Italian translation of the Spanish original, was published in Frankfurt a.M. The Spanish original, entitled *Picara Justina,* had been published in 1605 under the pseudonym of Francisco Lopez de Ubeda; its author was actually a Spanish Dominican monk by the name of Andreas Perez from León, a man who, both before and after publishing his *Picara Justina,* had also published several prayer books. He probably used the pseudonym in order to protect his reputation. Further German editions were published in 1626, 1646, 1660, and 1688; an additional second part was published for the first time in 1627. *Justina Dietzin* is of considerable importance for the German picaresque novel, insofar as Grimmelshausen also created a female counterpart to his *Simplicissimus,* namely, *Die Landstörtzerin Courasche.*

To summarize: The Spanish picaresque novel came to Germany in several stages and was assimilated in various ways. The following is a brief discussion of these stages: (1) The German *Lazaril von Tormes* was a direct translation of the original (1614); (2) Albertinus' *Gusman* was an already freely reworked and edited version, a sequel to the Spanish original (1615); (3) Ulenhart's *History von Isaak Winckelfelder vnd Jobst von der Schneid* substituted Bohemian conditions for the Spanish ones (1617). The sequence constituted by literal translation, an edited or reworked edition, and poetic assimilation signifies a rapid development, which demonstrates how German translators and editors strove increasingly to transform this new type of the novel into something unique—the expression of their own world. Thus, within a short period of time, the Spanish genre became a German one, although strong traits of their Spanish model can often be traced in the original German picaresque novels.[2]

Since the *Lazarillo* is the prototype of all succeeding picaresque novels, it can serve as a model for determining the criteria of the genre. As translations from the Spanish language constituted the genre of the picaresque novel in Germany for several decades, and since there is no original German novel which fulfills the requirements of the genre as perfectly as does *Lazarillo*,[3] it seems justified to use the Spanish novel as a model.

Born the son of a miller on the Tormes River in Spain, Lazarillo loses his father at the age of eight, when the latter is banished because he has embezzled grain. The father dies in a campaign against the Moors. Lazarillo's mother then lives with a Moor in Salamanca, who is later imprisoned because of theft. A blind beggar takes the boy along as a servant, but he allows him to go hungry and beats him mercilessly. Here Lazarillo learns to steal in order to stay alive. Lazarillo's second master is a priest in Maqueda, who deprives him of food to an even greater extent and almost beats him to death after discovering that the boy had stolen some bread. Lazarillo begs for alms in Toledo and gets as a third master, a nobleman who is unable to care for him, but who, in turn, must be kept by Lazarillo himself. He deserts the boy while fleeing from his creditors. Following this, Lazarillo serves a very worldly monk—a dealer in indulgences, who sells his merchandise by "arranging miracles." He also serves a painter and a captain, for whom he sells water in the streets, and after four years he obtains decent clothing. His service to a bailiff soon proves to be too dangerous, and he does not attain a peak of happiness until he becomes a public crier. His master, the archpriest of San Salvator, marries him to his maid and acts as his patron. Lazarillo refuses to listen to rumors that his wife is the archpriest's mistress. The German translation of 1614 adds a chapter from an anonymous sequel (Antwerp, 1555), in which Lazarillo makes the acquaintance of mercenaries of Charles V's army in Toledo. At this point, he expects a change of his fortune in the future.

A large number of picaresque qualities can be drawn from *Lazarillo*:[4] The picaresque novel can be termed a fictitious autobiography. The *picaro* relates his own experiences; therefore, the novel is written in the first person. This characteristic trait entails several consequences. For one, the distance between the reader and the narrator is shortened. By indirect address to the reader, this distance can even be completely suspended so that the novel becomes a direct dialogue with the reader. Even more important is the following aspect: an account of this narrative perspective, the *picaro* himself, as well as his entire environment, appears picaresque because it is viewed through the *picaro*'s own eyes. He recounts the events of his life, at the same time recollecting, describing, interpreting, and reflecting on it.

Consequently, the *picaro*'s entire outlook is one-sided. He has not only a limited point of view but also philosophical inclinations, and he draws from his own experiences general conclusions with regard to the nature of his surroundings. Indeed, the message of the entire book can be moralistic or didactic. For example, in the preface to the German *Lazarillo* translation, the fictitious *picaro* declares, with respect to the purpose of his narration, that his novel is an attempt to demonstrate how much more must be accomplished by a person who begins in extreme poverty and eventually gains modest means, as compared to someone who is born an heir to a great fortune (*LT*, p. 7). Short treatises and moralistic sermons and digressions of all sorts may also be inserted into the novel. This is not so much the case in the short *Lazarillo* as it is in Mateo Alemán's *Guzman*.

The structure of the picaresque novel is linear and enumerative. The narrator begins *ab ovo* with his own birth, possibly even with the events preceding it; he relates his parents' story and then narrates the sequence of the events constituting his own life, continuing in temporal succession until the conclusion of the novel. The novel does not always conclude with the narrator's present state; in many cases a sequel is promised—and this promise is often kept by subsequent and/or different writers. The enumerative narrative structure leads logically to an open conclusion. The alternative popular possibility for a conclusion is the *picaro*'s retreat from the world, by becoming a hermit, for example.

The enumerative character of the structure is strengthened by the account of the *picaro*'s experiences and actions: Lazarillo leaves one master for another, and in most cases he devotes one chapter to each of these masters. These individual chapters may, in turn, consist of several episodes of the merry-tale type. The chapter concerning the dealer in indulgences, for example, is in fact simply a merry-tale (*Schwank*). Lazarillo himself is not actively involved; he merely plays the role of a spectator. Very often individual episodes are interchangeable or can be omitted, although this interchangeability has often been overstressed in criticism of the genre. *Lazarillo*, for example, has a definite structural development. The hunger theme is increasingly intensified in the sequence beggar-priest-nobleman, and the last chapters show the "hero" on his way to ever greater success in life.

With the interchangeability of the episodes and the enumeration of merry-tale motifs, the picaresque novel greatly resembles the German chapbooks of the sixteenth century, for example, *Till Eulenspiegel*. This evidences a continuation of a German literary tradition.[5]

What qualities does this so-called hero possess? The *picaro* expresses so few heroic traits that he can only be termed the central character. According to his personal qualities he is rather an antihero, at least compared to the protagonists of the contemporary courtly-historical novel. The *picaro*'s parents belong to the lowest classes; they are thieves, prostitutes, and the like. Thus, the picaresque novel implies a sort of "hereditary" theory. In addition to this hereditary aspect, the milieu in which the *picaro* grows up plays a significant role. From the very beginning, he is forced to engage in a fierce struggle for survival. As a boy he serves various masters—in the case of Lazarillo, as a guide to a blind beggar, as an acolyte, or as a page. Very early in his career there is a turning point at which the *picaro* is transformed from a naïve boy into a cunning rogue, who tries to make his way by means of his wit and skill. This turning point takes the form of an experience which ingrains in him the hostility of his environment and makes him aware of the fact that he is completely on his own and has to fight. For example, Lazarillo is being cheated by the blind man, who hits the unsuspecting boy's head against a carved stone ox (*LT*, p. 13).

The *picaro* does not strive for riches but is primarily concerned with the preservation of his ever threatened physical existence, and secondarily, with a very modest subsistence, even if this life is suspect in the eyes of the world. The *picaro* is a cunning little scoundrel who lies, engages in petty thefts, and plays clever pranks, but he is by no means a plotting criminal. He commits most of his offenses more from impulse and need than from a desire for luxury and an easy life. He always remains the underdog, the scapegoat of society, thus securing for himself the reader's sympathy and compassion. In the picaresque novel, therefore, the emphasis lies on the material aspects of life, on its unpleasant side—on financial worries, privation, starvation, and the like. Consequently, detailed descriptions of objects and the material aspects of life abound. Nothing appears to be unworthy of description or mention; everything counts.

As has been mentioned, the picaresque novel is set among the lower classes. Its characters are beggars, fraudulent innkeepers, thieves, stingy or debauched priests, shabby, impoverished noblemen, quack physicians, and the like. Therefore, it is wrong merely to call the genre "realistic," because it does not mirror the whole spectrum of society but rather reveals the seamy side.

The picaresque novel affords a picture of the cultural and social conditions of Spain during the second half of the sixteenth century—a country which had become poor during this period—despite being at the peak of its power and despite the stream of gold that was flowing into the country from its colonies. The reasons for this impoverishment, in all probability, are the expulsion of the industrious Moorish population and the perpetual war conditions. The result was that the negative types of people as described in the picaresque novels actually existed in greater numbers than in other periods of history. A major feature of the picaresque novel is, therefore, its outspoken social and class criticism. Consequently, the characters often possess no individual traits; they are purposely represented as types. They do not have names and are characterized only by their profession or their social standing. In *Lazarillo*, we find, for example, such typical characters as the cunning beggar, the stingy priest, and the deceitful dealer in indulgences. By introducing the two latter characters, the author sharply criticizes conditions within the Catholic church. Also present is the typical figure of the impoverished Spanish *hidalgo,* the nobleman who proudly struts through the streets with enormous *grandezza,* bravely hiding his poverty and his growling stomach. Through this characterization a concept of honor, which was popular at that time but which is also masochistic and senseless is sullied: the nobleman preferred to leave his native village rather than to greet a distinguished neighbor.

As the characterization of the hero has already demonstrated, he is mainly concerned with physical survival and possibly with the attainment of a modest means of livelihood. The *picaro* is always aware of the fact that he is at the mercy of fortune, "the goddess *Fortuna,*" although he accepts his bad luck with amazing equanimity. The theme of the inconstancy of human life, which had been alluded to previously in the appended final chapter of *Lazarillo,* as well as the vacillation of the hero's fate, made it possible for this Spanish Renaissance novel to become the expression of German Baroque feeling and thinking. Thus, it was possible to transform the mere sequence of exterior experiences and social critiques, both of which features were maintained in the genre, into a well-structured novel with deep allegoric meaning.

II *Hans Jacob Christoffel von Grimmelshausen*:
Der abentheurliche Simplicissimus

Grimmelshausen's *Simplicissimus* is probably the best example of the extensive influence of the Spanish picaresque novel on the German novel of the same type in the seventeenth century. This novel also provides evidence of the change which the Spanish genre underwent in the hands of its German transformer, Hans Jacob Christoffel von Grimmelshausen. The complete title of the novel reads as follows:

Der Abentheurliche SIMPLICISSIMUS Teutsch / Das ist: Die Beschreibung deß Lebens eines seltzamen *Vagant*en / genant Melchior Sternfels von Fuchshaim / wo und welcher gestalt Er nemlich in diese Welt kommen / was er darinn gesehen / gelernet / erfahren und außgestanden / auch warumb er solche wieder freywillig quittirt. Überauß lustig / und männiglich nutzlich zu lesen. An Tag geben

Von GERMAN SCHLEIFHEIM von *Sulsfort*. Monpelgart / Gedruckt bey Johann Fillion / Im Jahr M DC LXIX.

The Adventures of a Simpleton. That is: The description of the life of a strange vagabond named Melchior Sternfels von Fuchshaim; where and how he entered this world, what he saw, learned, experienced and suffered there, and also why he voluntarily left it. Extremely entertaining and very useful to read. Edited by GERMAN SCHLEIF-HEIM von *Sulsfort*. Monpelgart. Printed by Johann Fillion In M DC LXIX.

Melchior Sternfels von Fuchshaim and German Schleifheim von Sulsfort are obviously pseudonyms. At the end of the sixth book of *Simplicissimus,* a person who calls himself H. I. C. V. G. P. zu Cernheim says that *Simplicissimus* as well as *Der keusche Joseph* and *Satyrischer Pilgram* were written by a man named Samuel Greifnson vom Hirschfeld (*ST*, p. [588]), who supposedly transformed his name anagramatically into German Schleifheim von Sulsfort. This is the key to the question of authorship of all three novels.[6] If one applies the principle of letter transposition or anagram to the signature and the date ("Rheinec. den 22. Apprilis Anno 1668"), "Cernheim" as well as "Rheinec" can be resolved into *Renichen,* an old form or the name of the village of *Renchen,* the *P(rätor)* and mayor of which, since 1667, was Hans Jacob Christoffel von Grimmelshausen (= H. I. C. V. G.). Correspondingly, all of the author's pseudonyms can be resolved into *Christoffel von Grimmelshausen,* including the name of the main character of *Simplicissimus,* which must be corrected to read *Melchior Sternfels von Fugshaim.* Apart from the fact that this playful rearrangement of letters probably indicates the author's belief in the instability and inconstancy of all earthly things, nevertheless the identity of author and the main character yields hints as to the autobiographical nature of the work.

In comparing the facts of Grimmelshausen's life and the contents of the novel, it becomes strikingly apparent just how many autobiographical elements have found their way into the novel. It would be wrong, however, automatically to arrive at conclusions concerning the poet's life from specific facts of the novel. Unfortunately, little concrete evidence exists regarding the life of Grimmelshausen.

The writer was a descendant of a formerly noble family of

artisans from the small city of Gelnhausen, where Grimmelshausen himself was born in 1621 or 1622. The story of his
childhood and adolescence cannot be reconstructed from official
documents. It has been concluded from the novel that young
Christoffel was kidnapped by Croatian troops, part of the Spanish army, in or about 1634, when they laid waste his home town.
In 1635 he was captured by Hessian troups and taken to Kassel.
Afterward he is thought to have been in both Hesse and Westphalia, as is evident from his intimate knowledge of the locale
and of various local personalities. In Westphalia all evidence
points to the fact that Grimmelshausen must have joined the
regiment of Count Götz, which took him to the border of
Württemberg in 1638/39. From 1639 to 1648 he was with the
regiment of Colonel Freiherr von Schauenburg, whose staff sergeant he was from about 1643 on. According to the Offenburg
parish register, he married on August 30, 1649, became manager
of the estates belonging to the Schauenburg family in Gaisbach
in the Rench Valley. Following that (1662-65), he became
castellan of the castle Ullenburg, which was in the possession
of Dr. Johannes Küffer, a fashionable doctor from Strasbourg,
who was very probably the model for the novel's unflatteringly
drawn Dr. Canard from Paris. From 1665 to 1667 Grimmelshausen was an innkeeper ("Zum silbernen Stern") in Gaisbach,
an occupation which probably provided him with the time and
opportunity to write. From 1667 on he was the mayor of Renchen,
his main tasks including the administration of lower jurisdiction,
the office of police chief and all the responsibilities of a notary
public and tax collector. During the following years he was
extremely active as a writer and published several volumes a
year. The financial rewards of this activity were undoubtedly
a welcome recompense for his natural urge to write. Grimmelshausen died in 1676 in Renchen, *honestus et magno ingenio et
eruditione,* as the parish register puts it. In all likelihood, the
poet was raised in the Protestant faith but later converted to
Catholicism.

The events of *Simplicissimus* show many parallels to this
curriculum vitae. Its contents may be briefly summarized according to its major subdivisions:

Book I: The hero is growing up in total ignorance, supposedly
as the son of a peasant in the Spessart mountains. His father's

44 GERMAN BAROQUE NOVEL

farm is suddenly attacked by looting soldiers, and the boy flees
into the forest, where a hermit takes care of him. He names the
boy Simplicius and instructs him in the teachings of Christianity.
Soon after the hermit's death, Simplicius leaves the forest and
comes to the Swedish fort Hanau, where the governor, Ramsay,
makes him a page.

Book II: Because of his foolish behavior Simplicius is made a
court jester, but he manages to preserve his sanity. Soon afterward he is kidnapped by Croatian troops, from whom he quickly
flees. He remains alone in the forest, living on food he steals
from farmers. By chance, he participates in a witches' Sabbath,
which he causes to disappear by invoking God. Serving again
as a jester in the siege camp facing Magdeburg, he makes the
acquaintance of both the older and the younger Herzbruder.
The older one becomes his teacher; however, he is soon stabbed
to death. The younger one, Simplicius' friend, is falsely accused
of theft, and must give up service in the army. Simplicius then
dresses as a girl and becomes a maid to a colonel and his wife.
Suspected of spying, he is imprisoned; however, the younger
Herzbruder frees him during a surprise attack. As the servant
of a stingy and simple-minded dragoon, Simplicius comes to
Westphalia into the monastery called "Paradise." After the
death of his master, he becomes famous as "Jäger von Soest"
("Hunter of Soest").

Book III: After having committed various kinds of pranks,
Simplicius is captured by the Swedes and brought to L. (Lippstadt), where he is granted complete freedom on his word of
honor. He courts a number of girls (leaving most them with
child), is forced to marry, and rides away to Cologne to retrieve
a treasure, which he had found previously and had entrusted
to a merchant there.

Book IV: As a chaperon of young noblemen, Simplicius comes
to Paris, and there he serves the fashionable doctor Canard.
He is successful as a singer in the royal opera and is able to
amass a considerable fortune by becoming a lover of wealthy
ladies. He flees, but all his money is stolen during an outbreak
of smallpox. He makes his way back to Germany, cheating
farmers as a traveling quack; however, he is caught and made
a musketeer in the fortress of Philippsburg. He is later freed
again by the younger Herzbruder, who, in the meantime, has

risen to high military honors. In a forest Simplicius meets the wicked Olivier, whom he recognizes from the camp at Magdeburg. Olivier is now living as a robber and relates his life to Simplicius. Soon afterward, he is killed by soldiers, and Simplicius involuntarily avenges his death. He is able to support the wounded Herzbruder with Olivier's money.

Book V: Herzbruder and Simplicius make a pilgrimage to Einsiedeln. Frightened by the devil, Simplicius decides to change his way of living. He accompanies Herzbruder to Vienna and there becomes a captain. Both are wounded, and they journey to a spa with a healing spring (*Sauerbrunnen*) in order to recover. Herzbruder dies, and Simplicius marries a country lass, continuing, however, to court other girls. He again meets his alleged father from the Spessart mountains and learns that he is actually the son of the hermit, a former officer of Scottish nobility who has become weary of the world. After visiting the Mummel Lake and its sylphic inhabitants and making a trip through Russia and Asia, Simplicius returns to his home and becomes a hermit on Mooskopf Mountain.

Book VI (Continuatio): Simplicius has a dream about a competition in Hell, between avarice and prodigality who ruin the wealthy Englishman Iulus and his servant Avarus. Leaving his hermitage in the forest, Simplicius becomes a pilgrim. In Egypt he is captured by robbers and is exhibited as a "wild man." On his way home, after he has been freed, his ship is wrecked in a storm, and only he and a carpenter are able to reach a paradise-like island. An Ethiopian woman who had been washed ashore turns out to be the tempting devil himself. The carpenter cannot resist the palm wine and soon dies. When a Dutch ship lands at the island, Simplicius refuses to return to Europe; however, he entrusts his life history, written on palm-tree leaves, to the captain for publication.

Following this summary, it hardly needs to be mentioned that Grimmelshausen was not brought up by a farmer in the Spessart mountains, nor by a hermit, that he was not married in Lippstadt, nor was he ever in Paris or even Russia, Asia, or the Middle East. It is also uncertain if he, for example, witnessed the Battle of Wittstock or the siege of Magdeburg. Descriptions of those historical events could easily have been related on the basis of oral or written reports and when the poet wants to move his hero from the area around Fulda to Magdeburg, he unhesitatingly transports him there by means of witchcraft— a means, which he himself questions directly afterward,—justifying it by "narrative" reasons (Book II, Chapter 18). However, these facts do not put the autobiographical character of the novel into question. Indeed, especially Books I-III definitely contain many events which are based on Grimmelshausen's personal experience. But a first glance at the contents brings to light just how many aspects of the genre tradition, historical sources, folklore, and literary *topoi* have been superimposed on the autobiographical core and have made the novel a work of art which, in essence, is truly fictional.

Grimmelshausen has borrowed purely factual information— descriptions of historical events as well as a large part of his scholarly discourses—from printed sources, either by rendering them literally or by modifying them slightly. His main source was an encyclopedic compilation by the Italian writer Thomas Garzoni, which was first published in 1585 in Venice. Grimmelshausen, who was, in all probability, unversed in foreign languages, utilized a German translation (first edition, 1619; second edition, 1669), entitled *Piazza Universale Das ist: Allgemeiner Schauplatz, Marckt und Zusammenkunft aller Professionen, Künsten, Geschäfften, Händeln und Handwercken,* and so on. His borrowings from this work are numerous; entire discourses, essays, as, for example, the discourse on the Merode= Brüder (Book IV, Chapter 13), have been more or less literally copied from Garzoni. Saints' legends are the basis of the novel's hermitages; and an originally Italian novella, which Grimmelshausen probably read in one of Harsdörffer's collections,[7] forms the basis for Simplicius' erotic escapades in Paris. Most of the "Stücklein," as Grimmelshausen calls the merry tales (the hero of which is Simplicius, for example as the hunter of Soest), can be traced back to the extensive sixteenth-century collections of merry tales. In describing battles, sieges, and other historical events, the former musketeer Grimmelshausen did not rely on his memory but consulted a monumental historical compilation of a seventeenth-century work entitled *Theatrum Europaeum.* In its numerous tomes, the historical events of the year directly previous to the publication of each volume were described in detail and were illustrated by numerous copper etchings. Coming upon this generous utilization of sources, it must be realized that a concept such as copyright was not yet legally enforced, so that unauthorized editions—also, for example, in the case of Grimmelshausen's writings—were the rule rather than the exception.

Serving as sources for *Simplicissimus* and, consequently, as models for the genre, were French picaresque novels as well as Spanish ones; the French had quickly adopted the genre. Grimmelshausen did not use material from *Lazarillo de Tormes* at all; but he did borrow from Ägidius Albertinus' adaptation of *Gusman de Alfarache*. Again, entire passages may be compared in order to demonstrate literal dependence.[8] In addition to *Gusman*, Grimmelshausen drew from the *Histoire comique de Francion,* a voluminous picaresque novel by the Frenchman Charles Sorel (1602-74), which only recently was proved to have been a source for *Simplicissimus.*[9] It cannot be our purpose here to compare the two works in order to establish a dependence. However, it is important to consider the question as to what elements the genre of the Spanish picaresque novel has contributed to *Simplicissimus;* to what extent Grimmelshausen remains within its tradition; and to what degree he has created something entirely new:

(1) The form of the autobiographical novel, with the hero narrating his own story.

(2) The technique of enumerating adventures, episodes, and merry-tale-like stories, of which Simplicius is the hero. This enumerative technique relegates Grimmelshausen's work to the tradition of the German chapbooks of the sixteenth century.

(3) The tendency to moralize, to insert entire discourses and moral treatises into the novel, a stylistic trait which Grimmelshausen adopted from Ägidius Albertinus.

(4) The general tendency to satirize and criticize one's own age. Both elements, often difficult to separate from each other, can be found not only in the Spanish picaresque novels, but also in Johann Michael Moscherosch's (1601-69) *Gesichte Philanders von Sittewald* (1643), whose vision "Soldatenleben" (soldiers' life) in particular is considered to have influenced Grimmelshausen's *Simplicissimus.* This, however, indirectly brings us back to the Spaniards, as the entire first part of Moscherosch's

work is more or less a translation of Francisco Gómez de Quevedo's (1580-1645) *Sueños* (first printing, 1627).

In conclusion, it can be said that in *Simplicissimus* Grimmelshausen has adopted numerous formal elements from the Spanish picaresque novel. As if to provide further proof of this fact, the character of the hero, Simplicius, is identical in many respects to that of the *picaro*. This similarity is not found throughout the entire novel, however, and certainly not in all situations, but it is discernible in many instances, as, for example, when Simplicius, as a page in Hanau, first becomes a victim of his colleagues' pranks. Like the *picaro*, he then gains his wits through the governor's attempt to change him into a fool. He even obtains a kind of superiority over the world, which enables him to be the hero of numerous pranks, as in the case of the *picaro*. Again, like the *picaro*, Simplicius is driven hither and yon by his destiny, that is, by the goddess *Fortuna*, who raises men to the peak of their happiness and then lets them fall again. Simplicius is a man in a sort of unhinged, unordered world, where anarchy rules and where each individual must protect himself and prove his own worth.

On the other hand, there are a number of characteristics which differentiate *Simplicissimus* from the picaresque novel:

(1) In sixteenth-century Spain, the setting for the picaresque novel, there certainly existed much poverty and moral decay, but it had not as yet reached the unparalleled proportions of the disaster of the Thirty Years' War in Germany. Such a background is entirely foreign to the Spanish picaresque novel.

(2) Both the Spanish picaresque novel and *Simplicissimus* follow the principle of recounting episodes, merry tales, and adventures; however, in addition to these features, *Simplicissimus* is firmly structured, even to a degree unknown in the Spanish picaresque novel, including *Lazarillo*. This definite compositional aspect also differentiates *Simplicissimus* from the German chapbooks.

(3) The hero's purpose and attitude, as intended by the author, display marked differences. The hero of the Spanish picaresque novel is concerned about suffering hunger, that is, physical survival. Simplicius, to be sure, finds himself in extremely difficult situations as well. However, the novel does not center around his material well-being, but rather on his spiritual state.

Christian religion continues to remain for him the binding religious and ethical standard, which he continually bears in mind, repeatedly measuring his own behavior by it. Simplicius does not merely accept his own fate but reflects on it and consciously interprets it. This lends an inner perspective to *Simplicissimus*, a reflective attitude which the Spanish picaresque novel does not display to such an extent.

In order to shed more light on the specific nature of *Simplicissimus*, all three of the foregoing points must be treated in further detail.

(1) *Simplicissimus* is considered *the* German novel of the Thirty Years' War. Indeed, one can go as far as saying that the present-day picture of the Thirty Years' War has been shaped by this novel. In it can be found descriptions of battles and sieges, of devastations of every kind, of looting soldiers who molest the farmers. Reports are given of farmers taking revenge on the soldiers, of life in the fortresses of Hanau, Philippsburg, and Lippstadt, and of life in the military camps. The general decay of moral values in the army, the facts about the foreign infiltration of Germany by France's à la mode culture, and so forth, are related. The novel is thus a mirror of the mores of its time and conveys to the modern-day reader the life of the people much more effectively than does any strictly historical account. Grimmelshausen offers this description of life, not so much in the role of a man of letters, but rather as someone who was a personal onlooker, who has actually viewed soldiers, burghers, and farmers, first as a young boy following the armies alongside the supply wagons and later as a musketeer and staff sergeant. Grimmelshausen depicts the various social classes and levels which are rarely encountered in the Spanish picaresque novels. *Simplicissimus* deals not simply with a cunning boy who is fighting against priests, noblemen, and vicious beggars, but presents farmers and soldiers as the main representatives of the people. In fact, Grimmelshausen's obvious compassion for the farmers, who carry the burden of the war, opens a new perspective in German literature. Up to this time, the peasant had almost exclusively assumed the role of the cheated fool of the Shrovetide play or the merry tale.

Moreover, the events of *Simplicissimus* and, therefore, of Simplicius' life, can be dated exactly. The Battle of Höchst

(June 10, 1622), in which Simplicius' father is separated from his wife (the determining factor in his father's becoming a hermit), has just taken place when Simplicius is born. The Battle of Nördlingen (September 6, 1634) forces the twelve-year-old boy out of the forest, following his stay with the hermit. The siege of Magdeburg places Simplicius between the two opposite types, Olivier and Herzbruder; and the Battle of Wittstock (September 24, 1636) releases him from military arrest. Other military encounters are simply mentioned in passing, and even the Peace of Westphalia (1648) is concluded practically unnoticed. On the whole, however, by referring to the historical events Grimmelshausen locates the action between 1622 and approximately 1650. Throughout, Grimmelshausen makes references to historical events, enabling the reader to establish an exact chronological sequence. Poetic freedom may be considered to be the excuse for small chronological leaps, or for the fact that sometimes in a short span of time more events take place than is reasonably possible.[10] However, in spite of this exact chronological placement of the events of the war and the detailed description of the mores of the time, *Simplicissimus* cannot correctly be termed a historical novel because Grimmelshausen never focuses on the events of the Thirty Years' War;[11] therefore, larger and more comprehensive historical perspectives are completely lacking, and historical events are mentioned only insofar as they affect Simplicius' destiny.

(2) It is virtually impossible to make a definitive statement about the structure of *Simplicissimus*. Since the beginnings of scholarship on Grimmelshausen a host of theories have been laid down, most of which are contradictory. The critics seem to agree on only one point; namely, the fact *that Simplicissimus* was structurally conceived and that it is *not* an unstructured, formless work. Therefore, a few representative theories will now be introduced, with the individual critics merely representing various schools of interpretation.

A theory dominant in the 1920's and 1930's was that *Simplicissimus* is an apprenticeship novel (*Bildungsroman*) or a development novel (*Entwicklungsroman*). For example, Friedrich Gundolf, who can be termed a typical representative of *Geistesgeschichte*, that is, an intellectual historian, came to the rather rash conclusion that the actual *Simplicissimus* (the plot shorn of insertions, digressions, and supplements) is clearly structured into sections dealing with simple-mindedness, folly, sin, punishment, and repentance.[12]

The attempt to make the five original books of *Simplicissimus* the basis of a theory concerning its structure was taken up by the Dutch scholar Jan Hendrik Scholte.[13] Scholte bases his theory on C. G. Jung's thesis that the structure of the classical drama, that is, its division into five acts, is an archetypal form of all human imagination and written expression, a concept which, according to Scholte, can also be applied to *Simplicissimus*. The first book, containing the hero's birth and upbringing, as well as the origin of the name "Simplicius," clearly has the character of an "exposition," the first encounter with the world at the governor's court being the "inciting moment" or "catalyst," according to Gustav Freytag's theory of the drama. In the second book, Simplicius is seen having a more expansive contact with the world. The contrast between his naïveté or simple-mindedness and familiarity with the ways of the world becomes embarrassingly acute, leading to main character's assuming the name "Simplicissimus," which demonstrates the so-called rising action. The third book, Simplicius as the hunter of Soest, is the "climax," followed by the "peripety" or "reversal" in the fourth book, as the amorous escapades of the stay in Paris end in poverty and sickness. The hero's life with Olivier represents—according to Scholte—the "falling action." The fifth book, in which the hero retreats from the growing number of experiences and travels in order to renounce the world, could then be regarded as the dramatic "catastrophe." The parallel to the father's life, also ending in a hermitage, adds a skillfully constructed symmetrical element to the dramatic construction.

This theory, which basically characterizes *Simplicissimus* as a development novel, contains a flaw in that it adds criteria which are foreign to the genre. Neither C. G. Jung's theory nor the terminology of Gustav Freytag's theory of the drama can be applied to a seventeenth-century novel, unless, by this token, any type of novel could be interpreted along these lines, which is, of course, impossible. Just how accidental, for example, the division of the novel into five books actually is, is demonstrated by the fact that Grimmelshausen added the *Continuatio* as a sixth book, which, as will later be shown, is an integral part of the entire novel. Indeed, Scholte's theory is partly responsible for the fact that he did not include the *Continuatio* in his critical edition of *Simplicissimus*.[14]

The denial of a unity of character with regard to the title hero, Simplicius, was the starting point for a critique of the thesis that *Simplicissimus* is a development novel. Now the main character was viewed as split into a series of distinct types. Johannes Alt is the chief representative of this school of interpretation. Like Jan Hendrik Scholte,[15] Alt believes in a symmetrical structure of the novel, with a gradual rise of the hero's "curve of good fortune," in opposition to which a descending moral curve must be imagined, the direction of the curves being reversed in the second half of the work. At the beginning of the novel, Simplicius is lonely, removed from the world, and destitute; at the midpoint he is wealthy and happy; and at the end he lives again in poverty, as a hermit. According to Alt, however, it is not the development of Simplicius' character, that is, of one individual, which is at stake, but rather a number of types (all of which are represented by the title character), one type following the next, in sequence. The delineations of the various types do not necessarily coincide with the beginnings and conclusions of the respective books but are located in the middle of the books, each midpoint being defined by a distinctive chapter containing a more general message. The following list represents, according to Johannes Alt's theory, the sequence of types in *Simplicissimus*, with the contiguous chapters serving as division markers: hermit (Bk. I, Chaps. 15-17: war tree); fool-Simplicius (Bk. II, Chaps. 17-18: trip by means of witchcraft); hunter of Soest (Bk. III, Chap. 14: capture); gallant adventurer (Bk. IV, Chap. 13: "Merodebrüder"); Olivier-Herzbruder (Bk. V, Chaps. 10-12: Mummel Lake); hermit.

This sequence-of-types theory must be criticized for several reasons.[16] The adherence to the principle of symmetry may turn out to be misleading, for such an approach carries a tendency to adjust the reality of the novel to fit the desired symmetry. Moreover, divisions between the types can by no means be found only in the middle of the individual books; and these types are in themselves not as homogeneous as Alt would lead one to believe. For example, the type "gallant adventurer" does not exist as one homogeneous unit; for the quiet, enjoyable life spent in Lippstadt (Bk. III) and the adventures of the quack physician and those of the musketeer in Philippsburg (Bk. IV), are fundamentally different. Furthermore, the hermitage episode at the beginning of the novel has very little in common with the corresponding attitude at the end. The beginning episode is of long duration, serious and emphatically religious; whereas the one at the end is defined merely by two half-sentences, which at the same time raise the question of the duration of the period spent as a hermit:

[...] daß ich die Welt verliesse / und wieder ein Einsidel ward: [...] / und fienge mein Spesserter Leben wieder an; ob ich aber wie mein Vatter seel. biß an mein End darin verharren werde / stehet dahin. (*ST*, p. 463)

[...] that I left the world and became again a hermit: [...] and started my life in the Spessart mountains again; whether I, however, will stay a hermit until I die, like my dead father, I have not decided yet.

The fact that in the character of Simplicius certain prototypes of literary heroes (such as the hermit, the fool and the adventurer, each one of which can be traced to a long international literary tradition) are incorporated is an obvious one and is not being questioned here. The parallels between Simplicius and Wolfram's Parzival, for example, are very striking.[17]

In fact, the question of literary traditions also yields certain results with regard to the inner structure of *Simplicissimus;* namely, if no attempt is made to devise a scheme for the structure of the novel as a whole, but rather to characterize the individual parts as generically determined in their own right. Clemens Lugowski has done this very successfully.[18] His point of departure is the famous story about the bacon theft. As the hunter of Soest, Simplicius is caught red-handed trying to steal a minister's meat provisions. By pretending to be the devil, Simplicius succeeds in escaping while the minister is exorcising "him." This story can be traced back to several sixteenth-century collections of merry tales. Within the framework of the novel surrounding it, it is autonomous, with a beginning and an end of its own. *Simplicissimus* contains quite a number of such short self-contained forms, which have their own independent existence in literary tradition, Simplicius being the hero of all of the tales, as were Eulenspiegel and the *Schildbürger.*

The action of the novel, therefore, serves as a skeleton for inserted independent literary material. These are not just merry tales. The life history of the wicked Olivier, for example, is closely related to the *exemplum,* because its main purpose is didactic and moralistic. Olivier's death, the logically horrible outcome of the *exemplum,* has been prophesied by the older Herzbruder, in addition to the fact that Simplicius was to avenge Olivier's death. The prophecies and their realization also represent an old narrative mold which had already been introduced in the ˙Hellenistic novel and which later became extremely popular in the courtly-historical novels of the seventeenth century. Prophecy and its realization span a considerable portion of the novel. This is also the case with another type of narrative. Persons are separated by some event, mainly misfortune, and they later meet again, seemingly by chance. Simplicius once more meets Olivier as well as his old foster parents. In this way, the beginning and the end of the novel are tied together.

An approach such as this one, which isolates independent literary genres and narrative forms, does not yield a theory about the overall structure of *Simplicissimus,* but it does isolate certain circumscribed formal units, demonstrating at least *one* of Grimmelshausen's techniques of composition.

(3) Once more, it is necessary to ask whether or not *Simplicissimus* is really more than a conglomeration of independent literary genres and narrative forms. Is not Simplicius more than a character who simply assumes the name of the hero of various "Stücklein" (pranks)? Friedrich Gundolf had already acknowledged that *Simplicissimus* does not deal with the life of a specific individual. He held, rather, that the poet may have envisioned presenting the symbolic or even allegorical history of any or all human life. The characters of the novel serve as bearers of ideas; this view is lent support (and thus far it has been undisputed on this particular point) by the function of two supporting characters, the good Herzbruder and the wicked Olivier, between whom Simplicius is placed as if between good and evil. They accompany him on his journey through life and reappear at every decisive point.[19] Olivier, on the one hand, represents the man who has fallen into earthly snares, who

adapts himself to the world and plays its game. Herzbruder, on the other hand, is the man who has remained untouched by the world and stands above mundane cares and worries; he does not make ethical compromises. Olivier's life history has a deterrent effect on Simplicius because in Olivier's life the final consequences of a worldly existence present themselves. The example set by Herzbruder repeatedly compels Simplicius to measure his own life by the standards of Christian morality.

Gundolf's viewpoint can also be accepted in seeing Simplicius as an exemplary character, a kind of test specimen who has been confronted with the world in order to demonstrate man's destiny and the true nature of the world. Simplicius has been placed in the world to try its moral character. He serves as a kind of measuring rod for worldly forces. As Simplicius, who stands between Herzbruder and Olivier, man is stationed between good and evil, between God and the devil. Without showing partiality to any denomination, Grimmelshausen wrote a basically religious novel, which describes man's struggle with the forces of good and evil. To be sure, Grimmelshausen also takes pleasure in writing as a craft; his main purpose in writing— his message—however, is a moralistic one. It cannot be denied that the author enjoys relating the "Stücklein" of his world-happy Simplicius; however, he concludes his book with the Spanish Jesuit Guevara lamenting about the world or, with Simplicius refusing to return to Europe (depending upon what is considered to be the actual end of the novel). In essence, the world is evil: that is the basic concept underlying the novel as a whole. Grimmelshausen justifies his thesis by presenting a *revue*-like series of experiences, that his exemplary hero undergoes.[20] He wishes to compel his readers to be critical of the world that surrounds them, to open their eyes to the ever-present danger of entanglement. There is no positive, that is, no *Christian* existence for his hero in this world. On this point, Grimmelshausen reflects the viewpoint characteristic of the gloomy spirit of the period of the Counter Reformation.

To return to the initial question—that of *Simplicissimus'* belonging to the genre of the development novel—it is obvious that at the end of the work Simplicius is not the same person he was at the beginning. The hermit on the Mooskopf mountain and the hermit on the island adhere to a vastly different philosophy of life than does the fool of Hanau or the hunter of Soest. Besides, the self-imposed hermitage at the end is, as has already been pointed out, not the same as the accidental hermitage of the young Simplicius at the beginning. Simplicius is now a different person, although he has not gained in wisdom by means of a linear or gradual development to a higher plane, as Gundolf posits, but through a more complicated process, vacillating between good and evil. His personal development can even be characterized as an almost spiral-like upward movement.[21] Admittedly, psychological continuity is lacking; there is no "individual" development in the modern sense of the word, as there is no actual "individual" as would be found in a modern novel. Consequently, all of the hero's adventures and encounters cannot serve as learning experiences. It must be realized that the character Simplicius is still a close relative of the "woodcutlike" characters of the sixteenth-century novels. After all, the "psychological" age with its soul-searching and its consciousness of individuality did not make its appearance until the eighteenth century, its prerequisite being sentimentality based on Pietism. Therefore, if terms such as "apprenticeship novel" or "development novel" are applied to *Simplicissimus*, then a work of a prepsychological era is described in terms which have been derived from products of the eighteenth and nineteenth centuries. For an apprenticeship or development novel implies the existence of an individual as a hero, his psychological development; he profits from his experiences, has a memory, and acts on the basis of what he has learned. However, another possibility is to define this type of novel from a historistic standpoint. In this case, a development novel may also be defined as a novel which presents an exemplary character in all his attitudes toward the world; there will be inconsistencies in the hero's behavior, but he will be continually conscious of the moral basis, or the lack of it, for his conduct, and at the end he will have to accept the consequences for his actions. Whether, therefore, one sees *Simplicissimus* as an apprenticeship or development novel depends on a definition of these terms.

The above discussion concerning the generic affiliation of *Simplicissimus* has merely served to offer a view of the complexity of the problem. Since the novel cannot be labeled in one specific way without excluding some of its features from the definition of the genre, an unequivocal identification with one particular genre will never be possible. However, a discussion of the problem can elucidate many aspects of the specific nature of the novel.

It is Grimmelhausen's primary interest to strip off the masks which the world has donned and to describe worldly matters as they really are. It is thus no accident that the frontispiece, a copper etching, depicts a monster which is part man, animal, bird, fish, and has the goat's horns of a satyr. In its hands it holds an open book which can only be interpreted as the book of life, as can also the objective symbols of the novel here depicted; a crown, a cannon, a tower, a goblet, a fool's cap, a set of dice, a sword, a ship and so on. There are masks lying at the feet of the satyr, and a poem is inscribed beneath it:

> Ich wurde durchs Fewer wie *Phoenix* geborn.
> Ich flog durch die Lüffte! wurd doch nit verlorn,
> Ich wandert durchs Wasser, Ich raißt über Landt,
> in solchem Umbschwermen macht ich mir bekandt,
> was mich offt betrüebet und selten ergetzt,
> was war das? Ich habs in diß Buche gesetzt,
> damit sich der Leser gleich wie ich itzt thue,
> entferne der Thorheit und lebe in Rhue.

> I was born out of fire, as was the Phoenix.
> I flew through air! but was not lost,
> I made my way through water, I travelled over land,
> by such journey I made the acquaintance
> of what often saddened and rarely gladdened me,
> what was that? I have set it down in this book,
> so that the reader may, like myself,
> avoid folly and live in peace.

In other words, the poet evinces a desire to remove the masks from the world, revealing its true nature, by having his hero experience it in its totality, which is hinted at by mentioning the four elements of fire, air, water, and earth. In addition, the poet stresses the moralistic-didactic character of his work. In the *Continuatio,* Grimmelshausen again makes the point that his style is satirical, according to the concept of satire acceptable to the seventeenth century. At first he apologizes that his subjects must occasionally be comic in nature. He states that he relies on humor only for the sake of those who can only swallow "sugar-coated pills" and continues:

Ich möchte vielleicht auch beschuldigt werden / ob gienge ich zuviel *Satyricè* drein; dessen bin ich aber gar nicht zuverdencken / weil männiglich lieber gedultet / daß die allgemeine Laster *Generali*ter durch gehechlet und gestrafft: als die aigne Untugenden freundlich *corrig*irt werden; [. . .] (*ST*, p. [472])

I might perhaps be accused that I am writing in much too satirical a manner; however, I cannot be blamed for that at all, because we generally tolerate much more easily that common vices are hashed over and punished than that one's own vices are corrected in a friendly manner; [. . .]

With this satirical style which characterizes his novel, Grimmelshausen definitely belongs to the tradition of the sixteenth and the early seventeenth centuries. Indeed, satire is Grimmelshausen's means of exposing the true nature of the world.[22]

The term "satire" may be defined very generally as literary castigation (*Stachelschrift*), as a censuring of the world's vices, as an unmasking of the evil and the unhealthy aspects of a time. This very general definition does apply at least to the seventeenth century. This fact having been accepted, *Simplicissimus* is satirical in several ways:

(1) In directly condemning various deplorable aspects of reality of the period, specifically the *alamode*-culture (Bk. I, Chap. 19), gluttony (Bk. I, Chap. 30), gambling (Bk. II, Chap. 20), and so forth. Directly after his arrival at Hanau, the young Simplicius, who has been taught unadulterated Christian standards, has the opportunity to make certain critical observations about human society, which he finds far removed from the true Christian spirit.

(2) As dream or visionary satire, for example, in the allegorical dream of the "war-" or "social-class tree" (Bk. I, Chap. 15), in which the poet sees mirrored the society at the time of the Thirty Years' War—a dream demonstrating the uselessness of the "little man's" striving and the corruption of powerful men, doubtlessly written under the influence of Moscherosch's visions. To this group also belongs the dream-allegory about avarice and wastefulness in the *Continuatio* (*Cont.*, Chaps. 2 ff.).

(3) As *verkehrte Welt* (world upside down), for example, in the description of Simplicius' foster father's farm (Bk. I, Chaps. 1 f.) or in the Mummel Lake episode (Bk. V, Chaps. 12 ff.).

(4) As Utopia, as in the episode about the German Hero (Bk. III, Chap. 4) or in the description of the life of the Hungarian Anabaptists (Bk. V, Chap. 19). Basically, the Utopias consist of a distinct realization of the principle of *verkehrte Welt*, because here the world is shown as it should be, whereas in reality everything is actually reversed.

The last two forms of satire need to be explained at greater length. As has already been mentioned, Grimmelshausen considers the world to be evil. He expresses this idea by means of the Baroque *topos* of *verkehrte Welt*. This can be defined as a world in which all standards have been turned upside down, in which the evil triumphs and the good succumbs, and where man attempts to do the opposite of what he should. In order to make this clear, Grimmelshausen causes his hero to be raised by the hermit, that is, to believe in a purely Christian standard, and then suddenly confronts him with the reality of the so-called Christian society in Hanau. Here Simplicius is bound to fail in assimilating himself. Since he feels and thinks like a Christian, he wants to act like one, and he assumes that everyone else shares his intentions. The principle is best demonstrated in the Mummel Lake episode (Bk. V, Chaps. 12 ff.), where Simplicius reports about life on earth to the king of the subterranean beings. Instead of giving a true account of reality, however, he draws a picture of ideal human behavior: the ministers are industrious; they avoid lustful living and the search for wealth; and their sole interest is in serving God and leading their fellow men along the path to Heaven. Rulers desire nothing more than justice. Merchants do not conduct business out of avarice but rather because they want to supply their fellow men with worldly goods; doctors are only interested in their patients' good health, and the like (*ST*, p. 427). The lack of truth in Simplicius' words is made obvious in the reward he is given: he is handed the stone which is supposed to create a mineral spring, wherever deposited, with the stipulation that he shall enjoy the spring in proportion to his revealing the truth (*ST*, p. 432). He promptly misplaces it and thus loses his "reward."

Grimmelshausen's Simplicius at times also depicts the world, not as it is, but as it should be. This evidences a manner of writing which the author repeatedly utilizes in the course of the novel and which, according to Lugowski's theory, constitutes an independent genre: the *Utopia*.[23]

(1) At the midpoint of Book III, that is, according to Johannes Alt, at a conspicuous point in the novel, Simplicius apprehends a fool who pretends to be the god Jove and prophesies that he, Jove, would send a "German Hero," who would restore religious unity, peace, and wealth; a secure governmental and social order, proliferation of the arts; and an overall strengthening of the German nation. It is, to be sure, a fool, who promises all this, who prophesies this future paradise, concluding his prophesies by suddenly attacking the fleas in his pants! Even if a certain amount of self-irony is involved here, it does not detract from the seriousness of the statements made. It is also a fool (Simplicius) who at the beginning of the novel is in possession of the correct standards.

(2) Simplicius sees the dream about a perfect human society fulfilled in the community of the Hungarian Anabaptists, so that he himself makes plans to establish a community of that sort on his own estate. His foster father from the Spessart mountains convinces him, however, that he would hardly find sufficient people for such an enterprise (*ST*, p. 441).

(3) The life of the Mummel Lake inhabitants must also be considered a Utopia. They have no conception of life after death, but they also have no knowledge of either sickness or sin in their life on earth. Among them harmony and mutual understanding prevail. It is characteristic for Grimmelshausen to state that these sylphs have sexual intercourse only in order to propagate their race and that they take no joy in sex. Basically this is a pessimistic Utopia, because obviously Grimmelshausen values this sinless society higher than the possibility of life after death.

(4) The *robinsonade* of the *Continuatio* can also be termed a Utopia; here Simplicius finally finds inner peace and expresses his refusal to return to Europe in the following words:

[. . .] hier ist Fried / dort ist Krieg; hier weiß ich nichts von Hoffart / vom Geitz / vom Zorn / vom Neyd / vom Eyfer / von Falschheit / von Betrug / von allerhand Sorgen beydes umb Nahrung und Klaydung noch umb Ehr und *Reputation*; hier ist eine stille Einsame ohne Zorn / Hader und Zanck; eine Sicherheit vor eitlen Begierden / ein Vestung wider alles unordentliches verlangen; ein Schutz wider die vielfältige Strick der Welt und ein stille Ruhe / darinnen man dem Allerhöchsten allein dienen: seine Wunder betrachten / und ihm loben und preysen kan; (*ST*, p. 584)

[. . .] here is peace, there is war; here I know nothing of arrogance, greed, anger, envy, jealousy, deceitfulness, trickery, of cares of all sorts, neither of sustenance or clothing nor of honor and reputation; here is a peaceful solitude without wrath, dissimulation or strife; a place secure from vain lusts, a barricade against all unsuitable desires, a protection against the many-sided hooks and barbs of the world, and a quiet calm, in which a person can serve the Divinity alone, observe His wonders and praise and glorify Him;

It is typical that, in these words, the ideal is expressed only by negating the prevailing conditions. Simplicius does not achieve inner peace before he finds himself on the lonely island, where the harmonious functioning even of a community of only a few people proves to be impossible.

By using these various forms of satire, Grimmelshausen castigates various deficiencies of the world, be they of a moral or of a material kind. Another failing of the world—a topic that permeates the entire novel—of which Simplicius' life is the prime example, is the *inconstancy* or transitoriness of everything earthly. This topic of permanence versus transitoriness has two sides. On the one hand, it plays a role within the hero; the stoic virtue of *constantia* (constancy) is a positive trait of the hero and one which he must prove he possesses. On the other hand, it plays a role outside the hero; as presented in the picaresque novel, the "world," human life, lacks constancy. In fact, the world is characterized by *in*constancy.

The moralistic aspect, *constantia* as a Christian-stoic virtue, is closely connected with the main problem of the novel, namely, the question: is a Christian able to remain such in an unchristian world, or is his corruption by the world inevitable? In order to prevent this process of corruption, the hermit father gives young Simplicius three rules to observe on his way through life, rules which, basically, mean the same thing, namely: remain constant: "Sich selbst erkennen / böse Gesellschaft meiden / und beständig verbleiben" (*ST*, p. 35). The entire novel is presented as a testing of the three rules—from which Simplicius deviates here and there—but which he never completely forgets, and he lives up to them at the end of the novel.[24]

The external ups and downs of Simplicius' life, the constant changing of his fate, are the heritage of the Spanish picaresque novel, which had previously attempted to express the transitory nature of the world. The symbol of this fickleness is the wheel of fortune of the goddess *Fortuna* which first elevates the hero and then lowers him back down into the depths of life (*ST*, pp. 224, 255, 327). Grimmelshausen makes frequent references to the changeability of fate. This topic completely dominates the *Continuatio,* the introductory poem of which is in itself a treatise concerning the transitoriness of the world:

> O wunderbares thun! O unbeständigs stehen
> Wann einer wähnt er steh / so muß er fürter gehen /
> O schlüpfferigster Standt! dem vor vermeinte Ruh
> Schnell und zugleich der Fall sich nähert zu
> Gleich wie der Todt selbst thut; was solch hin flüchtig Wesen
> Mir habe zugefügt / wird hierinnen gelesen;
> Worauß zusehen ist daß Unbeständigkeit
> Allein beständig sey / immer in Freud und Leid.

> Oh, awesome happening! Oh, ever-changing state!
> When one thinks he has come to a halt, he must proceed!
> Oh most vacillating condition! to which instead of the
> expected rest
> The fall is nigh; swiftly and imminently
> Just as death himself; what such inconstancy
> Has done to me, is to be read here;
> Which demonstrates that inconstancy
> Alone is constant, always in joy and misery.

When a cavalier sends his servant to ask Simplicius about his identity, Simplicius answers: "Mein Freund / sagt eurem Herrn widerumb / ich seye ein Ball deß wandelbaren Glücks; ein Exemplar der Veränderung / und ein Spiegel der Unbeständigkeit deß Menschlichen Wesens" (*ST*, pp. 534 f.). ("My friend, tell your master that I am a sphere of changeable fortune; an example of change, and a reflection of the inconstancy of human life"). This is a profound answer which, because of its insuitability to the occasion, can only be taken as an aid afforded by the author to the interpretation of the novel as a whole.

Besides the dream vision about avarice and wastefulness, the *Continuatio* contains two more allegories whose topic is inconstancy. In the first allegory, Simplicius takes a walk in the forest and comes upon the stone sculpture of "an old German hero" (*ST*, p. 505) which presently begins to move and talk to him. It introduces itself as Baldanders ("Soon-different"), a personification of transitoriness and change, which indeed can be said to characterize Simplicius' life up to that point. The statue tells him (*ST*, p. 506) that it had made Simplicius "bald groß / bald klein / bald reich bald arm / bald hoch bald nider / bald lustig bald traurig / bald böß bald gut / und in summa bald so und bald anders" ("now great and now small, now rich and now poor, now high and now low, now happy and now sad, now evil and now good, sometimes this way and sometimes that"), and that it would never leave Simplicius, whether he desired it or not. Baldanders then changes directly in front of Simplicius, first into a tall oak tree, then into a sow, then into a fried sausage, and suddenly into "peasants' dirt," into a beautiful field of clover, into a heap of cow dung (*ST*, p. 507), until finally it resumes human features, whereupon it flies away in the shape of a bird. The character of Baldanders is an invention of the German sixteenth-century poet Hans Sachs (1494-1576), but he used it only to serve to illustrate a principle, not, as in *Simplicissimus*, as a concrete character. The encounter in *Simplicissimus* is no blunt allegorical joke, since Simplicius comes face to face with the personified principle of his own existence.

Just as Simplicius, the hero, demonstrates the principle of the inconstancy of the world, so this principle is also demonstrated by a material object. In this case, it is a piece of paper hanging in a privy with which Simplicius converses. It relates to him the sad facts of its existence and the story of its life, from flax to cloth to paper.

After the transitoriness of the world has been demonstrated through the person of Simplicius and the objective world, and Simplicius has gone through various adventures, the robinsonade of the *Continuatio* makes its appearance, which is presented as the logical consequence of the world, the essence of which has just been allegorically summarized. Since permanence cannot be achieved within the world, Simplicius is taken out of the world (out of Europe) and is placed on a solitary island. Thus physically removed from transitory surroundings, he succeeds in defending himself from worldly temptations by means of his faith, and he is finally able to achieve the inner constancy of his own mind. Consequently, he has to reject the offer of being brought back to Europe. He is now in God's hand, removed from the realm of transitoriness.

The five books of *Simplicissimus* and the *Continuatio* (Bk. VI) have been treated as a unified whole. The new critical Grimmelshausen edition rightfully includes them in one volume. The interpretation of both parts as a unit is based on the final sentences of Book V, in which the hermit Simplicius voices uncertainty, asking whether he would remain in the wilderness until the end of his life, thus already hinting at the poet's intention of writing a sequel to his work. Indeed, at that very time Grimmelshausen was probably already working on the sequel.[25] The above interpreation has been an attempt to demonstrate that only by concluding the work with the *Continuatio*, not with Book V, can a satisfying and logical conclusion of the novel be attained. As we have also seen, the *Continuatio* is characterized by (dream) allegories to a much greater extent than was the case in the first five books of the novel, whereas the background of the Thirty Years' War is totally excluded. Also, whereas in the first five books the life history of Simplicius and that of Grimmelshausen are parallel in many respects, the *Continuatio* shows no such autobiographical tendencies.

Close together there are the allegories of the competition between avarice and wastefulness, of Baldanders and of the conversation in the privy. Simplicius' stay on the island is most interesting from the point of view of literary history and the history of genres, since the *Continuatio* contains the first German robinsonade before Defoe's *Robinson Crusoe* (1719). However, Simplicius' stay on the island does not represent a lamentable exile but an asylum, a retreat from the evil of the world. In writing this robinsonade, Grimmelshausen was inspired by a small work entitled *The Isle of Pines*, whose author was the English satirist Henry Neville.[26] The book was first published in 1618 in London and rapidly circulated on the Continent in the form of translations. Besides *The Isle of Pines* Grimmelshausen knew and extensively used a travelogue entitled *Orientalisches Indien*, which had been compiled by the brothers de Bry and had been published in a German translation in 1601 in Frankfurt. However, the fact that Grimmelshausen used printed sources is not as important as the way in which he used such material, the specific way in which he arranged the material. He borrowed many details in describing the island, the shipwreck, and so on. However, he did not write a satire of a travelogue, but rather an allegory, which—just like the other allegories of the *Continuatio*—summarizes the moral message of *Simplicissimus*, presenting it as a final intensification of climax. Thus, the ship's carpenter, who is washed ashore with Simplicius, represents the man who succumbs to temptation, whereas the Ethiopian girl represents temptation directly, the devil in person. The sailors who destroy Simplicius' cottage and garden stand for the eternal world, which intrudes into the isolation of the island. In the sailors' thinking, which revolves only around secular matters, they eat only the pulp of the fruits, which causes them to lose their minds; only by eating the seeds do they regain their health and sanity. That this unrealistic description has more than literal significance is demonstrated by the fact that Grimmelshausen applies the same metaphor to his own work:

[. . .] läst sich aber in dessen ein und anderer der Hülsen genügen und achtet deß Kernen nicht / der darinnen verborgen steckt / so wird er zwar als von einer kurtzweiligen Histori seine Zufriedenheit: Aber gleichwohl das jenig bey weitem nicht erlangen / was ich ihn zuberichten aigentlich bedacht gewesen; (*ST*, p. 473)

[. . .] if, however, someone is satisfied with the shell, disregarding the fruit which is hidden in it, he will surely derive satisfaction from an entertaining story, but he will not by far gain from it what I actually intended to prepare for him;

The sailors find pious proverbs and quotations from the Bible affixed to the trees, among others a mystical epigram:

Ach allerhöchstes Gut! du wohnest so im Finstern Licht! Daß man vor Klarheit groß / den grossen Glantz kan sehen nicht (*ST*, p. 537)

O highest good! you dwell in such dim light! That because of the great brilliancy, one cannot see the great splendor!

Correspondingly, the island hermit Simplicius can see the Divine truth only in the illumination given off by dead glow worms in the deep dark cavern. Thus, Grimmelshausen's most profound message is delivered in the form of a mystical allegory included in an allegorical robinsonade. Again this shows that the *Continuatio* must be the necessary sequel to, and conclusion of, *Simplicissimus*.

Grimmelshausen concludes his novel very skillfully by having the Dutch ship's captain, Jean Cornelissen, report about his ship's landing on the island and about his encounter with Simplicius. Through this narrative technique, not only is the illusion of the truth of the report enhanced, but the reader is, at the same time, more gradually removed from the autobiographical aspect of the novel. Through this stylistic device, the author artfully leaves the island hermit Simplicius behind. The occurrence of this masterful stylistic trait is not unique in the work. It has already been shown that Grimmelshausen must have had a clearly defined concept of a voluminous epic work as a whole. Accordingly, his mastery of this genre also shows itself in lesser ways in his style. His stylistic dexterity cannot be dismissed by merely labeling him a popular writer; to be sure, he often writes bluntly and with considerable humor, but he also masters the "keyboard of rhetoric," drawing on a stylistic tradition which can be traced back to classical antiquity. Although parts of the description of the Spessart farm are taken over from Garzoni (the description of it as a palace of nobility), the first chapters of the novel which contain this description are a rhetorical masterpiece of Baroque stylistics. Certainly the interspersed discourses may be considered monotonous today because they attempt to demonstrate the author's supposed book-learning with quotations from scholarly authorities. However, these parts are obviously intended to cater to the expectations and wishes of the general reading public of the times.

The entire manner of presentation, in addition, displays the satirical-moralistic character of the work.[27] Here, too, it becomes obvious that Grimmelshausen does not simply wish to entertain; he also continually attempts to serve didactic ends, so that the epic recounting of events or the merry tales are followed by moral discourses, giving them the character of *exempla* or moralistic examples. Thus, every event becomes a discussion of a paradigmatic case. Of course, there is also pure discussion in the form of discourses and didactic conversations—for example, with various ministers, with the older and the younger Herzbruder, and even with the wicked Olivier.

These didactic elements are matched by a humorous style of writing, which, as far as freshness and description of detail is concerned, is surpassed only by Johann Beer, in that it creates, before the reader's eyes, the full background of the Thirty Years' War. Naturalness and simplicity characterize this style. Keen observation of actual life is the basis for the manner of representation, which tends to dissolve every action experienced by the hero himself and seen by the reader through his eyes. This style, on the one hand, provides exact descriptions and, on the other hand, ironically interposes a distance from reality, for example, by describing the farm of Simplicius' foster father as if it were a palace of nobility. It does not lack proverbs, sayings of all kinds, dialect, descriptions of the filthy, nasty, and vile things of life; but at the same time it includes life's festive moments. Therefore, because of its close resemblance to actual life, it must be termed "realistic," in spite of its rhetorical estrangement. It is due to this popular, realistic style, which is in the tradition of the Spanish picaresque novel, that Grimmelshausen, in contrast to the writers of the courtly-historical novel, created a work which even today makes exciting reading.

III *Johann Beer:* Jucundus Jucundissimus *and* Die Teutschen Winter=Nächte / Die Kurzweiligen Sommer=Täge

About forty years ago, Richard Alewyn succeeded in attributing approximately twenty picaresque, satirical, and political novels, published under various pseudonyms, to Johann Beer, a musician at the court of Saxony-Weißenfels. Alewyn thus enriched the known body of facts about seventeenth-century writers by adding a new and very distinctive profile to their number.[28]

Johann Beer was born on February 28, 1655, in St. Georgen in the Attergau province of Upper Austria. Like Grimmelshausen and Abraham a Sancta Clara, the famed Baroque preacher, Beer, too, was the son of an innkeeper. Next to nothing is known about his childhood. He very probably left his parents' house at a very early age, living with relatives or as a page with several noble families. From the age of seven, he received musical instruction from the minister of his native village, and three years later he was accepted in the school of the Benedictine Abbey Lambach. A few years later, his parents moved to Regensburg, which was at that time the refuge of Austrian Lutherans, where from October 20, 1670, Beer attended the *Gymnasium Poeticum*. On account of his musical talents he was admitted to the *Alumneum*, a municipal boarding school, where he received free board and lodging. Having been granted a scholarship by the city of Regensburg, he began to study theology at the University of Leipzig in 1676; however, he terminated his studies after only one semester, entering the court orchestra of the Duke of Saxony-Weißenfels as an alto singer. A subsequent attempt to return to Regensburg was unsuccessful, and Beer, who did not feel at home in the petit-bourgeois world of the city anyway, remained in the freer world of the court, which had moved to Wießenfels, where he finally ascended to the rank of conductor. He was accidentally shot on a bird hunt and was wounded so badly that he died on August 6, 1700.

Beer was not only extremely productive as a novelist—his novels all appeared between 1677 and 1685—but he also became well known as a composer and as a musical theoretician. If one is familiar with the witty spirit of his novels, it is hardly surprising to learn that at his duke's table he often took over the function of a jester.

As in Grimmelshausen's case, we shall not attempt in the following to characterize all of Beer's novels; but rather to treat three picaresque ones which differ essentially in their fulfillment of the genre criteria: namely, *Jucundus Jucundissimus* and the two related novels *Die Teutschen Winter=Nächte* and *Die Kurtzweiligen Sommer=Täge*.

The plot of *Jucundus Jucundissimus* runs as follows: Jucundus is growing up in a remote valley of the Black Forest as the son of a poor brick-maker. A noble lady, who has been cheated and deserted by her husband and whose spoiled daughter has run away with a smith's hand, takes Jucundus with her and provides him with an education in her castle. Along with his private tutor, a student, he listens in prison to a murderer's life history. The prisoner turns out to be the noble lady's former husband. On the way to Jucundus' parents, his and his tutor's horses are stolen in a bewitched part of the forest, and, as guests in a castle, they are robbed of all their belongings. In the castle a hunter relates his adventures, giving special emphasis to his life as a page of a countess. After the two travelers discover that Jucundus' parents have passed away, they return home. During the winter in the castle they provide entertainment by having the peasants perform a comedy. The noble lady makes Jucundus her heir. He embarks on a vain search for a bride and ends up marrying the noble lady's daughter who, repentant, has finally returned home, having been saved from seduction by a fortunate accident.

The title shows that Beer has been greatly influenced by Grimmelshausen:

Jucundi Jucundissimi Wunderliche Lebens-Beschreibung / Das ist: Eine kurzweilige Histori Eines / von dem Glück / wunderlich erhabenen Menschens / welcher erzehlet / wie und auf was Weis er in der Welt / unter lauter abentheurlich= und seltsamen Begebenheiten herum gewallet / bis er endlich zur Ruhe gekommen / [. . .] Jedermänniglich / ohne Unterscheid des Standes / ersprießlich und nützlich zu lesen. (*JJ*, p. [67])

Fantastic life history of Jucundus Jucundissimus; that is: An entertaining story of a man strangely elevated by fortune; who tells how and in what manner he wandered through the world, encountering countless adventures and strange events, until he finally found rest [. . .]. Profitable and useful reading for everyone regardless of social standing.

This is an obvious imitation of the title of *Simplicissimus*. Just as in Grimmelshausen's masterpiece, in this novel, too, the son of poor parents, growing up in a remote mountain area, is removed from this environment by the accident of fate. The beginning and the end of *Simplicissimus* have influenced Beer's novels in several ways.[29] Indeed, Johann Beer is probably Grimmelshausen's only important successor.

However, what distinguishes Beer from Grimmelshausen is the structure of his plot. From the above summary it is clear that Beer's novel does not have a carefully planned overall structure, as is the case with *Simplicissimus,* no matter which theory is adhered to. Beer is exclusively motivated by what occurs to him on the spur of the moment,[30] by whatever comes to his mind while he is writing. His imagination embarks on flights of fantasy. It appears to run away with him, and he has trouble finding his way back to the continuing thread of the action. Consequently, he is very successful in setting the action of his novels in motion, but he has trouble completing the discussion of the topics introduced and in bringing his heroes' fate to a satisfactory end. It is typical, for example, that the skinner, with whom the noble lady's daughter has run away, is subsequently transformed into a smith's helper. Similar slips also occur in Beer's other novels. Without doubt, these novels must be read, not in terms of their totality, but in terms of each individual scene. Because of the compositional weaknesses, which often lead to an artistic weakening toward the end, Beer would hardly have been able to write a courtly-historical novel. The picaresque novel, with its open, additive form and with its popular style and milieu, was far more suited to his literary talents.[31]

Characteristic of Beer's novels are the inserted life histories. At the beginning of *Jucundissimus*, for example, the noble lady first, then the student, then the murderer in prison, and finally the hunter in the castle tell the stories of their lives. In these inserted stories we encounter genuine *picaros*. The student, who serves various masters as a private tutor, is a descendant of Lazarillo, for he too, has to struggle for his physical survival, being the servant of avaricious masters. The story of the murderer is similar to the life of Grimmelshausen's Olivier, with the difference, however, that the murderer in Beer's novel recognizes his own wickedness, thus making his autobiography appropriate to the character of a true *exemplum*. The hunter's adventures with the countess are, without doubt, influenced by Simplicius' erotic adventures in Paris.

However, what distinguishes Beer's *picaro* from the Spanish *picaro* or from Simplicius is the hero's success. The autobiographical narrator of *Jucundus Jucundissimus* encounters no serious problems during the course of his life. He does not become a symbol of inconstancy, tossed around by the goddess Fortuna. At the very inception of the novel he encounters a benevolent and wealthy lady who gives him a good education and finally makes him her son and heir. In contrast to the *picaro* of the Spanish novels, who is driven from master to master, as well as from one place to another, Beer's *picaro* is situated in one location to which he returns after short excursions. With the exception of these outings, he does not change his domicile during the entire novel. Thus, Beer's hero is a *picaro* only in the social sense—that of being a member of the lower classes, not in the sense of being a vagrant.[32] Jucundus lives the life of a young nobleman who is engaged in diverting himself during the monotony of winter. When he ventures out with his governor in order to seek a bride, elements of the political novel penetrate the superstructure of the picaresque novel. The actual picaresque plot is restricted to the inserted biographies, whereas the narrator, despite his picaresque birth, "arrives" socially, at the very beginning of the novel, and he encounters no serious problems for the remainder of the story.

There is another basic difference between Beer's *picaro* and Grimmelshausen's Simplicius: Jucundus is not a part of a plan of salvation. He does not represent man caught between good and evil, between salvation and damnation. His person does not serve to demonstrate how man can live in this world and at the same time be a Christian, as does Simplicius. Jucundus is, throughout, a worldly hero, whose relatively good behavior is more than adequately rewarded at the conclusion. His relation to God is not even discussed. Thus, Beer's *picaro* has taken on a definite secular color in comparison to Simplicius. Beer does not treat a moral or religious problem, but rather deals with life *in* and *of* this world. For this reason, his *picaros* are more closely related to their Spanish ancestors than to Simplicius. This holds true not only for a main character like Jucundus but also for the picaresque biographies of the supporting characters. The lack of fundamental or religious problems has its basis in the fact that Beer accepts the world as it is and holds the view that the world is basically good, whereas Grimmelshausen resoundingly condemns it, in the spirit of the Middle Ages or of the Counter Reformation (Guevara) of the seventeenth century. For Beer, there can be no doubt that a worldly life can be completely satisfying to man. In this connection it should not be forgotten that Beer comes one generation later than Grimmelshausen and, therefore, did not experience the Thirty Years' War. In contrast to Grimmelshausen, he led a rather entertaining and financially carefree life as a court official. By contrasting his novels with Grimmelshausen's, the considerable difference between the serious and rather melancholy early Baroque

period, during which Grimmelshausen as well as Andreas
Gryphius (1616-64) lived and worked, and the light, carefree
spirit of the late Baroque era, which encompasses the life
periods of Beer, Weise, and Reuter, becomes quite evident.

The unadulterated, positive attitude to worldly reality is
also evidenced in Beer's style. His superficial composition can
be considered the expression of his prolific imagination, of his
urge to invent fresh stories, which urged or compelled him,
every few pages, to devise new and original life histories or
merry-tale-like adventures and episodes. Beer's attitude to
reality reveals itself in his style, in his meticulous description of
reality, to an extent which is hardly ever encountered, if at all,
in Grimmelshausen's writings. When, at the very beginning of
Jucundus Jucundissimus, the reader is taken into the cottage of
the brick-maker, Beer commences by relating in detail the
financial troubles of the family, how these problems arose, how
the noble lady had an accident with her horse, a description
of the room, what is being served for dinner, and so forth. The
vividness of the description in Beer's picaresque novels is by
no means counteracted by rhetorical devices, so that his style
can be more correctly termed "realistic" than can Grimmelshausen's.[33] Every line evidences the author's enjoyment in his
narration; this enjoyment is found perhaps to a greater extent
in the case of Beer than in that of any other Baroque poet.
Beer conducts his narration out of a natural urge, from a need.
His purpose in telling stories is to entertain his reading audience,
not to instruct them or to improve their morals. Indeed, it can
be surmised that many of his stories were originally communicated orally to his friends. It is obvious that his written style
is more or less identical with his spoken style. The source of
Beer's prolific narrative capacities is seen, then, not as serving
moralistic-didactic purposes, as was the case with Grimmelshausen, but rather in serving his own inner satisfaction, for the
pleasure he derived from telling stories.

Grimmelshausen and Beer share a negative opinion concerning women: Beer as well carries the standard antifeminism.
In *Jucundus Jucundissimus* this becomes obvious by the fact
that women are introduced into the stories as objects of seduction or as criminals. Beer's women are considerably more subject
to their sensual desires than are his men. Their overwhelming

tendency is to seduce men and to commit crimes; rarely does the reader encounter good housewives, and they are, in most cases, only briefly mentioned since their uneventful existence offers precious little entertainment for the reader. When Jucundus searches for a wife, an unseemly female specimen is presented, mainly because she serves to personify, in one being, a wealth of physical deficiencies. The fact that the protagonist finally marries the noblewoman's daughter who ran away with a skinner's or smith's helper does not help to restore the honor of the female sex. This development was simply motivated by the attempt to bring about a positive conclusion, for the reason that Jucundus must be allowed to prosper in life.

Among Beer's novels, his so-called *Reiferomane* (novels of artistic maturity) definitely have a higher literary value; they are often referred to as Willenhag-novels: *Die Teutschen Winter=Nächte* and *Die Kurtzweiligen Sommer=Täge,* in which Beer, in epic proportions, employs the full array of his narrative talents and artistry. The two novels are clearly related. Although the characters have different names in the two novels, their identity as one set of characters is still quite obvious.

Very little can be said concerning the plot of the two novels, as there is no story line with a beginning and an end. A group of country noblemen form a brotherhood for purposes of mutual support and entertainment. They visit one another, celebrate all kinds of festivities, play pranks on one another, temporarily retreat into the wilderness in order to try out the life of a hermit, fall in love, marry, raise families, and hire their household servants, who relate to them their life story, and so on. Altogether, there is a merry potpourri of entertainment and social togetherness. Beer is not interested in describing the development of his characters or changes brought about in them by their experiences; rather, he is interested in capturing the peculiarity of the specific moment. In short, he is interested in events rather than in people. What he narrates is not world history but subjective events and personal experiences. Historical facts are, at the most, marginally mentioned, and it can only be concluded from remarks which the characters make that the action is supposed to take place during the generation in which the poet lived. Only the former soldier Krachwedel appears as a relic of Simplicius' time. Otherwise, all associations with "the great world" are consciously avoided.[34]

The locale of the action is Upper Austria. This conclusion can be drawn not only from numerous names but also from the number of crucifixes standing by the roadside, the statues of Mary, and the monasteries and castles. In general, Beer describes the landscape in which he spent his own youth. He introduces a page, who commences to tell the story of his own life as follows:

DIe Oberösterreichische Landschafft ist eine unter denen Vornehmsten des Teutschlandes. Ihre herrliche *Situation* / und die gesunde Lufft haben sie allenthalben / noch mehr aber ihre schöne Gebäude / bekannt gemacht / (*KS*, p. 326)

The province of Upper Austria is among the most splendid of Germany. Its magnificent location, its healthful air, and even more, its beautiful buildings have made it famous.

With the following passage, the page continues this description in detail, until the point at which he begins to talk about himself:

Ich bin alda / [. . .] was meine Geburt betrifft / in dem Adergey / etwann eine Stund von Ader=See in dem Marckt St. Georgen gebohren / welche unter die Graffschaft der Kevenhiller gehörig. (*KS*, p. 329)

I was born there, [. . .] if you are interested in my origin, in the Adergey about one walking hour from the Ader=lake in the village of St. Georgen, which belongs to the counts of the Kevenhills.

It must be remembered that Beer, too, was born in this area, and how many autobiographical experiences his novels contain can only be speculated about. In retrospect (he had left his homeland at the age of fifteen), he may have idealized the recollection of his homeland, but a true profile of Upper Austria definitely emerges in the Willenhag novels.[35]

In *Jucundus Jucundissimus* the manor was introduced as the principal place of action. This is even more strikingly the case in the Willenhag novels; here the noblemen visit each other on their estates and their castles, spending their time in an innocuous social life. Yet it is questionable if Beer was able to describe the Upper Austrian nobility *realistically*, since he had known it only as a child. This, in addition to the fact that a description of life at court, that is, of the poet's immediate surroundings, is lacking in his novels, leads the reader to suppose that Beer is rendering an ideal depiction of his own dreamings with seemingly realistic features. His ideal is, then, the independent country nobleman, who, free from financial worries, can live his life, following his own inclinations:

Rechtschaffen gelebet / seinem Nächsten guts gethan / darinnen stehet die wahre Vollkommenheit. Ein Gläßlein Wein mit einem guten Freund auszu *poculi*ren / ist keine Sünde / [. . .] (*KS*, p. 57)

To live like an honest man doing good for one's neighbor; that is true perfection. It is no sin to empty a glass of wine with a good friend, [. . .]

With these words one of the noblemen summarizes the ideal of his own life, a view which may justly be recognized as the one Beer himself held. This carefree social life is basically all that is found in the Willenhag novels. The brotherhood of noblemen does not have to prove itself up to meeting any emergency; it encounters no crisis but only extolls social togetherness in celebrations of all kinds.

The two novels have about two hundred characters; about one hundred are in the mainstream of the action and constitute the upper narrative level. The characters can be classified in two groups, differing in social positions at birth, in wealth, and social independence:[36] (1) the group of the established, wealthy country noblemen; and (2) the group of poor, unsettled, vagabond-type soldiers, students, pages, and the like, who temporarily find refuge in the castles of the noblemen; in brief, *they* are the actual *picaros*.

At times in jest the noblemen assume the function of the *picaro*, except in this case Beer has substituted a settled existence for the vagabond life and substituted sensual pleasures for the struggle for physical survival. In addition, the individual *picaro* is replaced by an entire group of noblemen. The autobiographical narrator, von Willenhag, does not serve as a dominating main character but reports the activities of the group of his friends. As in *Jucundus Jucundissimus*, the actual picaresque biographies, however, are found in narrations of the pages, horsekeepers, and old soldiers. The old master seems to be on very friendly terms with these people of lower social standing, treating them almost as his friends.

Whereas in *Jucundus Jucundissimus* the picaresque existence is seen through the eyes of an "almost-*picaro*," in the Willenhag novels it is from the standpoint of the country nobleman, who listens attentively to the narrations for pure enjoyment.[37] In fact, there are two avenues of entertainment for the reader; he is entertained by the merry-talelike events of noble country life, and he shares with the nobleman the amusements of the *picaro* tales (which occupy a considerable part of the novels). Since the main action takes place among the upper social strata, and since the actual picaresque world unfolds socially beneath the plane of the narrator, a complete reversal of the social perspective is witnessed.[38]

In contrast to *Jucundus Jucundissimus,* the Willenhag novels are not entirely free of ascetic elements, which have already been encountered in Grimmelshausen's *Simplicissimus.* The hermit motif recurs, for example, through the friends' temporary retreat from the world; they merely "act" as hermits. But what color do these periods of hermitlike existence take on? The narrator himself tries to be a hermit at the beginning of *Sommertäge* by first retreating to a chamber in his castle's tower, then by having a hermitlike gown tailored for him, and finally by having the walls of his domicile coated with bark, in order to re-create, artificially, at least, the adequate local color. The Scotsman Friederich, the most serious of the friends, is haunted by ghosts during his hermit period, thus contributing a pleasant ghost story, the type which Beer must have believed himself. Afterward, Friederich falls in love and marries. Another member of the group has food sent to him from his castle's kitchen during his hermitlike retreat, reads books, and makes music. That kind of contemplativeness has little to do with a renunciation of the world as is found, for example, in Grimmelshausen's *Continuatio.* The hermit's life has been degraded to the level of a social game, one which is being acted out the same way as going on a hunt or taking on courtly or municipal services would be.

It is typical for Grimmelshausen that his renunciation of the world is characterized by the Simplician "Adieu Welt," closely following Guevara, the Spanish Jesuit of the Counter Reformation. Beer, too, draws from authority for his renunciation of worldly life: The hermit Willenhag reports in *Sommertäge* that he has translated Thomas à Kempis' book *De Imitatione Christi* for his own edification. Two chapters of this translation have been inserted at the beginning and at the end of *Sommertäge*.[39] Whereas Guevara's renunciation of the world, however, can be considered a radical one, Beer's Thomas à Kempis gives advice of a much more moderate nature:

es ist sehr nützlich / daß der Mensch / er seye wer er wolle / zuweilen eine gelegene Stunde suche allein zu seyn. (*KS*, p. 11)

it is very profitable that a man, no matter who he is, try once in a while to be alone for an hour.

Whereas Guevara preaches ascetic renunciation, indeed, even contempt for the world, Thomas simply extolls self-discipline and contemplation *in* this world.[40] Friederich, too, presents his arguments in this spirit, thus making himself the mouthpiece of Beer's philosophy of life, which he advocates in his novels:

Der Mensch ist ein Thier / zur Gesellschaft geschaffen / und solches wird vielmehr uns adelichen Leuthen anstehen / weil wir / als eine Fackel / dem andern Pöbel zu leuchten / vorgesetzet sind. Es ist gar gut / daß man sich denen eusserlichen Welt=Sorgen zuweilen entziehe / damit man desto gefasster an einem einsamen Orthe seine innerliche Angelegenheiten behertzigen kann. Aber es ist darumben nicht nöthig / alle eusserliche Gesellschaft auf ewig zu fliehen / sondern nur auf eine Zeit seiner Amts=Geschäffte sich [. . .] zu enteussern / [. . .] (*KS*, p. 24)

Man is a social animal and especially we noblemen have an obligation to be sociable, because we enjoy our privileges in order to set an example for common people. It is good that one occasionally withdraw from external worldly worries so that one may the better care for one's inner self at some solitary place. But in order to achieve this it is not necessary to flee human society forever, but only that one free oneself temporarily from all obligations.

Beer is by no means consistent in his motivation for adopting a hermit's life. At the end of *Sommertäge*, the narrator, who has again become a hermit, hints that he does not know whether he wants to stay in the forest or would prefer to change his life style again (*KS*, p. 404); this should probably be interpreted not only as a borrowing from *Simplicissimus*, Book V, but also as being in accordance with Beer's general views regarding a hermit's life.

It is especially difficult to judge Beer's literary merits and his achievements in the history of German prose because his discoverer, Richard Alewyn, has already given him a rank equal to Grimmelshausen. Certainly a comparison of the two writers is warranted and has been attempted above in several instances, but it must be realized that the two writers belong to two different generations having differing intentions with regard to the creation of a novel. This explains why Grimmelshausen is definitely superior to Beer as far as depth of thought and compositional planning are concerned, whereas Beer exceeds his predecessor as far as his farcical humor, the fruits of his vivid imagination and his creative fantasy are concerned, as well as in the arrangement of individual scenes and in providing pure entertainment. Without questioning the justification of Alewyn's praise and the importance of his discovery, this writer would rather agree with Manfred Kremer, who summarizes his judgment by stating that Beer, without a doubt, is a great literary *talent* but no *genius*. In comparison with Beer, Grimmelshausen proves not only to be a great poet but also a profound thinker.[41]

IV   *Christian Reuter*: Schelmuffsky

With the exception of Grimmelshausen's *Simplicissimus*, Christian Reuter's *Schelmuffsky* is probably the only German seventeenth-century novel which is still popularly known today and appreciated among a wide reading public. Numerous popular and several scholarly editions bear witness to this fact.

The novel appeared first in 1676, anonymously (version A), then in the same year in a revised version under the pseudonym E. S. (version B). E. S. probably stands for Eustachius Schelmuffsky. Not before the end of the nineteenth century could it definitely be proven that the author was Christian Reuter, then a student in Leipzig. Reuter is an author typical for the end of the seventeenth century, insofar as he was just as unorthodox as was his novel. His life can be compared to that of Christian Günther or Christian Friedrich Hunold, all of whom are authors who, going beyond the traditional style of the seventeenth century, were no longer public servants, diplomats, theologians, or schoolteachers with a fixed salary. Reuter's *curriculum vitae* can only be reconstructed from the minutes of trials, parish registers, student registers, and the like, and the written accusations against him have to be evaluated with special care.

Christian Reuter was baptized the son of a farmer on October 9, 1665, in Kütten, a parish in the vicinity of Halle a.S. We know practically nothing about his childhood. At the beginning of the winter semester of 1688, he is found a law student in Leipzig, where he had been rooming since 1694 with his friend, Johannes Grel, in an inn called *Zum roten Löwen,* the owner of which was a widow by the name of Anna Rosine Müller. The two friends presumably led a rather unsettled life; they were certainly not "academic bluestockings."[42] Since their landlady was unable to secure any rent from them, she eventually threw them out.

At the end of the seventeenth century it had become fairly customary to take revenge on one's enemies by writing a *pasquillo,* thus exposing them to the ridicule of the general public. For example, Johann Beer inserted all sorts of invectives and insults into his novels, and Hunold made his novels even more insulting. Reuter, too, used these tactics: In October, 1695, his first comedy was published under the title: *L'Honête Femme / Oder die / Ehrliche Frau / zu Plißine / in Einem Lust-Spiele / vorgestellet / und / aus dem Französischen / übersetzet / von Hilario.* For the citizens of Leipzig it was not very difficult to recognize the Müller family and their inn behind the characterizations: the female protagonist, Frau Schlampampe, with her standard saying, as reprinted in the frontispiece ("So wahr ich eine ehrliche Frau bin"—"As sure as I am an honest woman"), her son Schelmuffsky, so fond of traveling, and the inn, now called *Zum goldenen Maulaffen* were all identifiable. Promptly the widow Müller instituted legal proceedings against Reuter and Grel at the University Court, and Reuter did not gain much by claiming Molière as his model. As the single originator of a *pasquillo,* he was suspended from the university for two years after a pretrial imprisonment of fifteen weeks. Reuter, who was under orders not to write any further *pasquillos* and not to leave the city of Leipzig, did not follow this injunction. In 1696 he not only published his novel *Schelmuffsky* but also a comedy entitled *La Madadie & la mort / de l'honnête Femme / das ist: / Der ehrlichen Frau Schlampampe / Krankheit und Tod*, followed in 1697 by *Letztes / Denck= / und Ehren-Mahl / Der /weyland gewesenen / Ehrlichen Frau Schlampampe*. The widow Müller had died on June 3, 1697, and on July 31 Reuter was incarcerated because of breaking orders and soon afterward was suspended from the university for six years, a punishment that terminated his academic career. In 1700 he obtained a position as secretary of the chamberlain von Seyfferditz in Dresden. From about 1703 on he was employed as a court poet of the first Prussian king, Frederick I, in Berlin. He died around 1712.

The subject of *Schelmuffskys Wahrhafftige Kuriöse und sehr gefährliche Reisebeschreibung Zu Wasser und Lande* is a fictitious trip allegedly taken by Frau Schlampampe's son Schelmuffsky, who had already bragged about his extensive travels in *Die Ehrliche Frau*. Since his mother was frightened by a rat, who had eaten holes in her silk dress, Schelmuffsky is born prematurely. Until the age of twelve he is brought up entirely on goat's milk. Having stayed at home until the age of twenty-four without learning a trade, he sets out on a trip accompanied by a "count" ("der Herr Bruder Graff"). In Hamburg he fights a duel for the sake of the lady Charmante; then he has to flee to Stockholm because he has wounded an entire gang of rowdies. The count follows him there. On a trip to Holland, their ship is wrecked in a storm, but the two friends swim a distance of one hundred miles to Amsterdam, clinging to a board. There they receive the highest honors, in spite of their indecent behavior. The count dies from excessive heat on a trip to India. There the Grand Mogul offers Schelmuffsky the position of State Chancellor on account of his knowledge of arithmetic, but Schelmuffsky prefers to return to London where again he has considerable success with women. On a trip to Spain he is captured by the famous pirate Bart and is imprisoned in St. Malo, from where his mother releases him for a ransom of one hundred talers.

In the second part of the novel, Schelmuffsky returns to his mother in Schelmerode in rags, but is unable to find her home

or to speak his mother tongue. On a subsequent trip he comes to
Venice, which (in this novel) is located high atop a mountain,
and Padua, where he lodges in the inn *Zum Roten Stier* and
encounters a family resembling his own. From there he travels
to Rome, where he defeats the pirate Hans Bart. On his way
home he is robbed of all his belongings in the Black Forest
and again returns home in rags.

Reuter has reworked the first, shorter version A into the
later, longer version B for artistic reasons.[43] The difference between the two versions is primarily linguistic. The language of
B is more vivid, and it employs more realistic metaphors. It
prefers the more specific picture to the general adjective. The
words selected are more extreme in meaning; indicators of
place, time, and number are more specific, and objects are
described more carefully. The stereotyped formulas are more
frequent—for example in Schelmuffsky's frequently interjected
phrase "der Tebel hol mer" ("the Devil take me"), and in
stories, such as the one about the rat, which are repeatedly
told in a leitmotiv manner. On the one hand, Reuter utilizes in
B more dialect and commonplace language; on the other hand,
he also uses more French words. He does this to demonstrate
by means of language the contrast between Schelmuffsky's crude
behavior and his social pretensions, since Schelmuffsky does not
write polished literary German but recounts his life in his
spoken language version. A is basically a travelogue which
gradually moves its characters from place to place and from
station to station; whereas B is primarily determined by Schelmuffsky's character, who in constantly new situations betrays
the contrast between his bourgeois-peasant birth and his noble
pretensions. In B, explanations for Schelmuffsky's feelings and
motivations for his actions have been included. Again and again
it is demonstrated how strongly the hero is convinced of the
value of his own person and to what extent he is interested
in maintaining the image of his allegedly high birth, and his
untarnished reputation. The other characters are secondary to
Schelmuffsky. They have the sole purpose of mirroring or empha-
sizing his character. Karl Tober[44] has well summarized the difference between A and B by saying that in A the contrast
between bourgeois behavior and noble birth is expressed in one
direction specifically: Schelmuffsky wants to compete with the

nobility by setting out on the grand cavalier's tour and becoming a mendacious traveler. However, the second version is more than a fictitious travelogue. For in this instance the contrast between a coarse bourgeois fellow and a noble dandy is developed within Schelmuffsky and is reflected in all his actions.

The second part of the novel also makes it very clear that, actually, Schelmuffsky has not taken any trip at all. His insolent little cousin simply laughs at him when he says good-bye and insinuates that Schelmuffsky would probably get no farther than to the next village, where he would convert his inheritance into brandy and tobacco (S, p. 93). The second part of version B also contains the ingenious trick of having Schelmuffsky face himself. By calling the boasting son of the innkeeper of the *Roter Stier* in Padua a liar, he actually criticizes his own personality (Chap. IV). This satirical device of self-unmasking by confrontation with one's own double makes this scene much more important than the mere fact that in the innkeeper and her family it is possible to recognize Reuter's former landlady. Schelmuffsky is an artistically designed character, who is so much a product of his author's imagination that such similarities become totally irrelevant. In addition, the first part of the novel does not contain any simulations of the Müller family. Thus, *Schelmuffsky* is no longer a *pasquillo,* as are Reuter's comedies, but because of the characterization of its hero it has become a literary work of art, which far excels Reuter's other works.[45]

Reuter's preface, entitled *An den kuriösen Leser,* suggests the interpretation of the novel as a persiflage of contemporary travelogues:

Es hat der Tebel hol mer mancher kaum eine Stadt oder Land nennen hören, so setzt er sich stracks hin und macht eine Reisebeschreibung zehen ellen lang davon her, wenn man dann nun solch Zeug lieset, (zumal wer nun brav gereiset ist, als wie ich [Schelmuffsky] so kan einer denn gleich sehen, daß er niemals vor die Stubenthüre gekommen ist. (S, p. 5)

Certain people, may the Devil take me, have barely heard a city or country mentioned, then they sit down and write a travelogue about it, ten feet long. Now, when you read such stuff (especially someone who is well-traveled such as I [Schelmuffsky]), you see right away that he never set a foot beyond his doorstep.

The seventeenth century produced a large number of travelogues, describing foreign countries and strange customs, foreign
rulers and their courts, adventures on the sea, and battles which
enraptured the German burghers who had stayed at home. This
type of literature was to gain new popularity with the advent
of the many versions of Robinson and other adventurers of literature at the beginning of the eighteenth century. To be sure, the
element of persiflage played a role in Reuter's writing of *Schelmuffsky*, but the author certainly did not focus on it.

One's attention is drawn to the character of Schelmuffsky
who constantly claims respect imitating courtly behavior on the
one hand and the realistic aspect of the rustic bumpkin on the
other. This contrast always shows through, finding its best
expression in the juxtaposition of the two levels of language.
This makes *Schelmuffsky in part* a satire on the German burghers
who at the turn of the century continually strove to reach
above the limits of their class. It is hardly accidental that the
protagonist sets out on a cavalier's tour which was considered
part of the education of a young nobleman; not by chance does
he always introduce himself as a nobleman, notwithstanding
the fact that his true character comes to the fore in all his words
and actions.[46] However, Wolfgang Hecht has convincingly
demonstrated[47] that Reuter intended to ridicule not only the
burghers but also the German nobility of the last decade of the
seventeenth century. For example, Schelmuffsky's traveling companion, the alleged count, is not a courtier but a dunce, who
consumes brandy by the gallon, hosts whole armies of lice in his
pants, and behaves just as coarsely as Schelmuffsky himself.
Hecht is of the opinion that in his negative description of the
world of high society, Reuter probably came rather close to
reality. That the rural nobility was decadent and pleasure-
seeking to that degree can easily be verified by the picture
drawn of it in Johann Beer's novels. In other words, what at first
glance appears to be Schelmuffsky's subjective world and the
product of his imagination is much more realistic than one tends
to believe if one simply listens to the braggart. In fact, Schelmuffsky himself unconsciously describes actual conditions. This
double meaning not only provides the comic effects in the novel
but also, at the same time, its various satirical aspects. Reuter
does not *only* criticize the burghers who attempt to rise above

their own class, but also the nobility, and thus the whole outgoing Baroque culture, whose courtly character was gradually waning by the end of the seventeenth century. What Opitz, Gryphius, and Lohenstein recognized as ideals, Reuter could no longer take seriously.[48] Again, Tober correctly summarizes the situation[49] by saying that Schelmuffsky presents himself to the reader as the caricature of a life style that has by this time lost its meaning. Reuter criticizes the world around him. He condemns the lust for drinking bouts and scuffles, the appeal of foreign cultures and titles—indeed, even excessive praise of the home country. He ridicules the struggle of the burghers to rise above their own social class as well as educational journeys. In *Schelmuffsky* the personal satire, the *pasquillo* of the Schlampampecomedies, has turned into the satire of the society of the waning seventeenth century.

If one interprets *Schelmuffsky* in this way, that is, as the ridiculing of courtly Baroque culture, one can no longer view its hero as a descendant of the *milites gloriosi* of Andreas Gryphius (*Horribilicribrifax*) or of Duke Heinrich Julius von Braunschweig (*Vincentius Ladislaus*);[50] this type of the Bramarbas (the bragging soldier) is being spoofed by the courtly society's revelation of his pretended courtliness. This courtly society's ideals are, in this type of comedy, the generally recognized norm. But in *Schelmuffsky* it is precisely this norm that is being ridiculed. In addition, Reuter's novel does not demonstrate any contrast between the braggart and the court; rather, Schelmuffsky exposes himself by his own behavior and by his narrative style. His character is not only far more realistically drawn than that of the *miles gloriosus*, who carries the heavy burden of a long literary tradition. In addition, the traditional soldier-braggart is, in most cases, a real nobleman—during the seventeenth century more probably an officer who served in the Thirty Years' War—whereas Schelmuffsky is a simple burgher.

It is frankly impossible to tag *Schelmuffsky* with the label of a specific type of novel. Here, too, a general syncretism of the types of German novel at the turn of the century is noticeable— a phenomenon that will have to be taken up later on. Just as the attempt has been made to view *Schelmuffsky* as the parody of a travelogue or simply as a tall tale, it has also been viewed as a late brother of the picaresque novel.[51] This is justified at least with respect to the external composition. As is the case with the picaresque novel, *Schelmuffsky* is subdivided into short chapters which, in rapid sequence, relate various adventures of the hero. The action proceeds in one single stream, the individual scenes following one another like beads on a string. Other features which *Schelmuffsky* has in common with the picaresque novel are that Schelmuffsky's life is told from his birth, that it is a constant up and down, without his ever complaining about this fact, and that the hero does not seem to grow older and apparently enjoys eternal youth. Although the *picaro* knows more tricks than Schelmuffsky, who is a dunce, both end their lives in poverty.

What, on the other hand, sets *Schelmuffsky* apart from the picaresque novel, is the hero's demand for respect as a person of rank; it is the demand of his ego, the foolhardiness of a self-confident ignoramus. In *Schelmuffsky* there are no moralistic or didactic insertions or scholarly essays, as, for example, are to be found in *Simplicissimus*.[52] This points to another difference between this work and the picaresque novel. The *picaro* was basically only a means of demonstrating the true nature of the world, that is, of reality per se. Thus, he constitutes a character with a specific function. Schelmuffsky, however, does not express the religious aspect of the *picaro* existence. His stories are neither merry tales nor simply comic episodes. What makes them amusing and entertaining is, rather, the way in which he relates them. Schelmuffsky is no longer a Baroque type; he is a character in his own right, that is, a genuine individual. The Baroque hero in him has been destroyed by satire. It is the special literary achievement of his author, Christian Reuter, to have created this multifaceted individual. Reuter is no great figure in German literary history, but because of his inclination to ridicule Baroque culture, he belongs among the forerunners of the German Enlightenment. He is part of the changing scene of European culture around 1700.

Due to its literary value, *Schelmuffsky* has had the greatest effect of all of Reuter's works on other poets.[53] During Reuter's lifetime the novel hardly seems to have been known outside Leipzig, but at the end of the eighteenth century it doubtlessly served as a model for the elaborate title of Gottfried August Bürger's (1747-94) *Münchhausen,* one of the greatest German collections of tall tales. The complete title reads: *Wunderbare Reisen zu Wasser und Lande des Freyherrn von Münchhausen* (1786).[54] In 1792 a sequel to *Schelmuffsky*, which is now lost, was published. It was the circle of the late Romanticists around Achim von Arnim and Clemens von Brentano who became enthusiastic about the novel, an enthusiasm shared by Joseph von Görres and the brothers Grimm. The circle around Brentano was strongly influenced by *Schelmuffsky* until about 1813; phrases, expressions, and allusions to that novel set the tone of their conversations and the style of their letters. The reason for their enthusiasm about *Schelmuffsky* was not merely confined to the interest which they took in older German literature, however. They felt a relationship with the spirit of the hero, who was creating an entire world around himself through his imagination and his flights of fantasy. Thus, already in 1807 Schelmuffsky was a character in Brentano and Görres' *Geschichte von Bogs dem Uhrmacher*. In Arnim's *Wintergarten*[55] there appeared a version of the novel which was censored (for female readers) and condensed to about twenty-five pages, and in Brentano's essay *Über den Philister vor, in und nach der Geschichte* the following was stated:

Es gibt mir keine schärfere Probe der Philisterei als das Nichtverstehen, Nichtbewundern der unbegreiflich reichen und vollkommenen Erfindung und der äußerst kunstreichen Ausführung in Herrn Schelmuffskys Reise zu Wasser und zu Lande.

There is for me no more accurate test of Philistinism than not understanding, not admiring the incomprehensibly rich and perfect invention and the extremely artistic presentation in *Herrn Schelmuffskys Reise zu Wasser und zu Lande*.[56]

V   The Political Novel
Christian Weise: Die drei ärgsten Erznarren in der ganzen Welt

The word *politisch* ("political") is a vogue word, employed in the seventeenth century, much like *galant* and *curiös*.[57] Christian Weise especially employs it frequently, not only calling one of his novels *Der politische Näscher*, but also composing a rhetorical guide entitled *Politischer Redner* and a guide for letter writing entitled *Politische Nachricht von Sorgfältigen Briefen.* *Politisch*, however, is a very ambiguous term. In the age of the Baroque, the term *politicus*, its Latin equivalent, was applied to the following types of people: (1) "gallant" people in general; (2) flatterers and office-seekers, who were always on the lookout for their own advantage; and (3) all secular officials, lawyers in particular; men of the world in general.

Whereas the second definition emphasizes its negative connotation, a concept that had become very popular following the Spanish Jesuit Balthasar Gracián's *Handorakel*,[58] the third definition stresses the personal dexterity and abilities of an active man. In Zedler's *Universal-Lexikon*, the most comprehensive German encyclopedia of the first half of the eighteenth century, the following appropriate definition is found:[59]

Das ist ein wahrer Politicus, welcher vermöge seines munteren und mit einem wohlgeübten Judicio verknüpfften Ingenii sich gegen die Güter, die als Mittel zur Erlangung der unmittelbaren Güter dienen, als Ehre, Reichthum, Gemächlichkeit, geschickt verhält, und seine und anderer äußerliche Glückseligkeit auf eine rechtmäßige Art zu befördern weiß.

A true *politicus* is he, who by means of his alert genius, combined with a good sense of judgment, is skillful in applying the qualities which serve to obtain the immediate rewards such as honor, wealth, and comfortable station, and who knows how to further his own happiness and that of others in a legitimate way.

In other words, *politisch* is identical with "worldly"; a *politicus* is a man of the world.

It is now necessary to determine the nature of a *political novel* by taking as an example Christian Weise's novel *Die drei ärgsten Erznarren*, since Weise is commonly considered the originator of the political novel—a type of novel which, one the one hand, shares several characteristics with the picaresque novel and which, on the other, differs from it in the narrative intent and in its bourgeois ideology.

In viewing Weise's life, it becomes readily apparent that this man, unlike Grimmelshausen, who had a relatively unsettled youth, would not attempt to write about the ever-changing life of a *picaro* but rather about those didactic and bourgeois elements which ultimately did find a place in his novel.

Christian Weise was born in 1642, the son of a professor at a *Gymnasium* in Zittau/Silesia. From 1660 to 1663 he studied theology, philosophy, law, and medicine in Leipzig, acquired an M.A. degree, and afterward lectured on ethics, history, rhetoric, and poetry. He did not succeed in obtaining a professorship and became the secretary of Count Simon Philipp von Leiningen in 1668 and, later on, the private tutor of young noblemen. In this capacity he had the opportunity to rid himself of all academic pedantry and to acquire, in its place, modern, courtly-cosmopolitan manners. In the summer of 1670 he became professor of rhetoric and poetry at the *Gymnasium* in Weißenfels, and in 1678 he became the principal of the *Gymnasium* in his home town, Zittau, where he remained until the end of his life (1708).

Weise's literary productivity was enormous. He presented about sixty school plays (*Schuldramen*) to posterity, most of them comedies, in which he dramatized biblical, historical, and literary themes. In addition, he produced all types of lyric; numerous theoretical writings dealing with rhetoric, ethics, religion; and a cycle of novels consisting of four works: *Die drei Hauptverderber in Deutschland* (1671), *Die drei ärgsten Erznarren in der ganzen Welt* (1672), *Die drei klügsten Leute in der ganzen Welt* (1675), and *Der politische Näscher* (1678, but written before *Erznarren*).

Weise was a burgher and an educator at the same time, and both bourgeois and pedagogical elements are present in his novels. During the course of the seventeenth century, an important social change had taken place in Germany. In the second half of the century the courts were still the main cultural and social centers, but the states, whose administration was becoming increasingly complex, could be governed only with the aid of expert officials and civil servants who had to be recruited from the burghers. It was, therefore, extremely important for a burgher to acquire an education, which then enabled him to compete for these high administrative posts. This was not achieved by training in scholastic philosophy but by acquiring much-needed foreign languages; a basic knowledge of law; some familiarity with the constitution and the administrative system of one's own and other states; a knowledge of geography, history, rhetoric, science; and, above all, a command of courtly manners, which included riding, fencing, and dancing—on the whole a worldly practical education, which would prove to be useful in public and political life. Because of his own comprehensive education and in his experiences in living in courtly circles, Weise felt compelled to put these ideas of a political education to practical use. After becoming the principal of the *Gymnasium* in Zittau, he soon transformed it into one of the most advanced and progressive schools in Germany. Officially, he did not change the curriculum, which demanded oral and written command of Latin; he did, however, in special, private courses (which soon outnumbered the official ones) teach his students geography, genealogy, history, ethics, politics, and physics. It should not be forgotten that in the seventeenth century enormous progress had been made in the field of the natural sciences and that "experience," "experiment," and "empiricism" were terms which people were becoming more and more conscious of—they were applying scientific reasoning to other areas of life as well.

Weise's novels served to supplement his educational intentions, which were to be more fully demonstrated in his novel *Die drei ärgsten Erznarren.* In his preface to the novel Weise shows his intention of giving instruction. He rejects *Simplicissimus* and other "old-fashioned" books (*lederne Salbader*), as well as pornographic literature (often camouflaged as satire), quoting as an example the infamous *Klunckermutz.* His own work he praises as a "possierliche *Apothecker=Büchse*" ("an entertaining remedy"), which would perhaps have more influence on some people:

als wenn ich *Catonem* mit grossen *Commentariis* hätte auflegen lassen. Plato hat gesagt: Imperare est legitime fallere populum. Es scheint als müste man die Tugend auch *per piam fraudem,* der kützlichten und neubegierigen Welt auf eine solche Manier beybringen, drum wünsche ich nichts mehr, als die Welt wolle sich zu ihrem Besten allhier betriegen lassen. Sie bilde sich lauter lustige und zeitvertreibende Sachen bey diesen Narren ein: wenn sie nur unvermeckt die klugen Lebens=Regeln mit lesen und erwegen will. (*E,* pp. 3 f.)

than if I would have published *Cato* with an extensive commentary. Plato said: *Imperare est legitime fallere populum* (To rule means to cheat people legitimately). It seems as if one had to teach virtue *per piam fraudem* (by means of a pious fraud) to the frivolous and curious world in such a manner; therefore I do not wish anything any more than that the world would allow itself to be cheated here for its own best. It may imagine all kinds of comic and amusing things in viewing these fools: if only it inadvertently reads, and considers the prudent maxims as well.

In his last will, a wealthy nobleman demands from his heir-to-be, the nobleman Florindo, that he commission a painter to depict the three biggest fools of the world in a hall of his inherited castle. This stipulation has only one intention: before Florindo can accept his inheritance, he must view the world and, by his search for the fools, thereby educate himself. So he sets out with his tutor Gelanor, his witty administrator Eurylas, who functions as the quartermaster, and with a painter. Everywhere—in the stagecoach, in the inns, at the lunch table, visiting towns and villages—the travelers are able to acquaint themselves with the most varied sorts of people and witness their follies. They encounter fools of love, slaves to fashion, braggarts, impostors, misers, would-be scholars, and so on. The travelers are almost exclusively observers and only occasionally become involved in the action. Gelanor, the tutor, adds in most cases a moralistic-didactic commentary to the observations, pointing out the general significance of what has been witnessed.

With this parade of fools, which forms a kind of unsystematic "fool's catalogue," Weise stands in the tradition of the *Narrenrevue* (collection of fools), as was first completely developed in Sebastian Brant's *Narrenschiff* (1494). Brant's work was imitated several times during the sixteenth century. However, Weise departs from this literary tradition by adding the motif of the journey and, above all, by not abstractly listing individual follies. In certain cases, he has people tell their entire life history, to exemplify wrong behavior. One example of this is seen in Chapter VI, where the travelers overhear three old gentlemen relating their life stories to each other: The first one has wasted his fortune on unnecessary travels and by participating in the expensive life at court; the second has wasted his life as a soldier; and the third has squandered his paternal inheritance by being idle and spending money foolishly.

From Moscherosch, Weise has taken over the pretext under

which he commences his *revue*: In the first vision of the second part of *Gesichte Philanders von Sittewald,* entitled "A la Mode Kehrauß," a dying king sends his inexperienced son out into the world to present a golden apple to the greatest fool. As happens later on in Weise's novel, the motivation is to give the "hero" greater experience in life and more worldly wisdom. Just like Weise's Florindo, the King's son is accompanied by an intelligent tutor, who from time to time must restore the prince's proper perspective. This theme of having the inexperienced person accompanied by an intelligent guide is also utilized in the narrative frame of Moscherosch's *Gesichte,* in which the unsuspecting Philander is accompanied by Expertus Rupertus, his experienced mentor, exactly as takes place in Dante's *Divine Comedy.* As already mentioned, these are elements of the dream allegory, another tradition in which Weise is writing this novel.

Some picaresque novels also show a *revue* character, especially the French ones; for example, Charles Sorel's *Francion* (1622) and *Polyander* (1648) or Johann Beer's *Narrenspital* (1681) in Germany. Here the hero's adventures are, to a large extent, only a means of introducing the various kinds of fools, for example, "fools of love," crazy poets, *milites gloriosi*, courtiers, or alchemists in an array of loosely connected scenes.[60]

Critics have repeatedly attempted to view Weise's novels in the tradition of Grimmelshausen, for in Grimmelshausen's novels[61] as well the heroes are guided through the world with the purpose of showing the world to the reader. This is, for example, the case in *Simplicissimus.* However, the two parts of *Das wunderbarliche Vogelnest* are much more similar to Weise's novel. The decisive difference lies in the fact that Grimmelshausen allows his heroes to experience the world merely in order to demonstrate to them—and to the reader—how sinful, wicked, and fundamentally evil it actually is, in an attempt to bring his heroes and his readers back to God. Weise, too, reveals the follies of the world; however, unlike Grimmelshausen, he does so with the intention of educating both and of preparing them *for* the world. Whereas Grimmelshausen held a passive, pessimistic attitude toward the world, Weise's attitude is aggressive and optimistic. In his writings, the Baroque condemnation of the world is rejected. Whereas in Grimmelshausen's writings the Christian religion is still the point of reference and the criterion for judging human actions, Weise still bases the principle of his moral on the Christian religion, but a man's actions are primarily seen in connection with secular public life and are judged by the standards of worldly society.

This task of searching for the three greatest fools is already part of the literary tradition of the impossible tasks, which can be found repeatedly as early as in Greek legends (Paris) and in folk literature (fairy tales). In Moscherosch's vision the golden apple is not presented to anyone. Weise arrives at a forced solution, which both points back to the religious basis of his ethic, still prevalent in his writings, while at the same time, however, it contradicts the spirit of the novel. If one wants to be exact, the novel has several conclusions. After viewing all the fools, a decision must finally be made as to who the three greatest fools really are. In Chapter XLVII, the entire task is first concluded in a humorous, ridiculous solution by the painter posing the question to the servants and receiving the answer that the greatest fool is the one who would pose such a question at all (E, p. 217). This episode constitutes in itself a merry tale, but it prefaces a more profound statement. One of the servants adds:

Ein jeglicher Mensch ist ein Narr, aber der wird ins gemein davor gehalten, der es mercken läst. Ja sagte der Mahler, der es mercken läst, der ist gar ein kleiner: aber der sich vor klug hält, der ist viel grösser, und wer an den beyden seine Freude hat, der ist der allergröste. (E, p. 217)

Everyone is a fool, but generally he who shows that he is is he who is considered to be one. Indeed, said the painter, he who shows it is a bit of a fool, but he who considers himself clever is a greater one and he who laughs at both is the greatest of all.

Indeed, the three fool seekers prove to be fools themselves, above all the painter, who is made fun of over and over again, and Florindo, who engages in a senseless duel (Chap. II), and who, even at the end of the novel, is still dispatching bombastic love letters to his beloved at home. Thus he falls into the category of the most extreme "fools of love." The tutor Gelanor states, at the beginning of Chapter XLVIII, with reference to the painter:

ICh sehe wohl [...] das Reisen hilfft nicht wider die Thorheit. Es mag einer in Franckreich und Italien gewesen seyn, so heist es doch mit ihm: fleucht eine Ganß hinüber, kömmt eine Ganß wieder herüber. (*E*, p. 221)

I see very well [...] that traveling is no remedy against foolishness. Someone may have been in France and Italy; yet the saying still applies: Once a fool, always a fool.

This statement may very well be considered ironical and applies to the other travelers as well.

Gelanor, who believes that he is able to locate the three greatest fools, is forced, at the end, to beg from a *Collegium Prudentium* to reveal the true meaning of folly and what the greatest folly is considered to be (*E*, p. 216). It seems to contradict the entire spirit and intention of the book to consult, at the end, a learned society, that is, theoreticians, for advice, after the travelers' common sense has utterly failed to furnish a solution. It is not surprising that the society returns a very general answer, concluding:

Nun ist leicht die Rechnung zu machen, wer der gröste Narr sey: Nemlich derselbe, der umb zeitlichen Kothes willen den Himmel verschertzt. Nechst diesem, der umb lüderlicher Ursachen willen entweder die Gesundheit und das Leben, oder Ehre und guten Namen in Gefahr setzt. (*E*, p. 226)

At this point it is easy to decide who the greatest fool is: namely, he who forfeits heaven for the excrements of this world. Following him; he who for wanton reason endangers either his health or life, or his honor and reputation.

As a result, the three spaces in the hall of Florindo's castle are decked with three pictures, each of them depicting a man embracing a woman whose rear aspect displays fire (hell), a skeleton (death), and a beggar woman (honor, reputation). Above these pictures there are corresponding inscriptions in Latin, ascribing the quality of emblems to the pictures. Whereas the journey of the fool seekers was geared toward practical experience, at the conclusion of the novel there is the theoretical conclusion of a learned society, which places eternal values above temporal ones, and there are different versions of the emblematic representation of *Frau Welt* ("Lady World"). Instead of this being a view forward into the eighteenth century, it is a look back into a Baroque, ascetic way of thinking; indeed, with the resumption of the *Frau Welt* motif, it signifies a leap back into the Middle Ages. Within the novel—for example in Chapter XXI or XXIX—Weise, on several occasions, criticizes scholasticism and its meaningless discussions. The fact of his conclusion seems, if not to renounce this criticism, at least to question its credibility by returning to methods which he himself criticizes within the novel.

The reader of Weise's novel finds himself in a peculiar situation. Either he can consider the allegorical representation of the alleged three greatest fools and the report of the academy as Weise's conclusive remark about the problem, in which case he adheres to an artificially supplied moral somewhat poorly conceived by the author. Or, on the other hand, the reader may consider the travelers to be positive examples, possibly his own models; he will have trouble doing that, as well, however, since the painter is a comic character, and Florindo himself embarks on the greatest of follies. At the most, the reader can accept the guidance of Gelanor's comments, whom Weise has obviously made his own mouthpiece in many instances. Gelanor can be viewed, then, as an impersonal, rationalizing commentator of factual situations rather than as a true character of the novel. From these commentaries the reader can definitely profit, being enlightened by Gelanor-Weise on the individual follies of man. However, this also demonstrates the weakness of *Die drei ärgsten Erznarren*: the lack of a coherent plot as well as of rounded characters, which makes it questionable whether or not a work of this kind should be termed a novel.

Weise himself, and the literary critics after him, decided to call a work like *Die drei ärgsten Erznarren* a *political novel* ("politischer Roman"). A political novel is supposed to educate the reader for a successful bourgeois life in this world, to make him beware of folly, stupidity, and intellectual pretense of any kind, to bring him to understanding, to a recognition of himself and the possibility of his own betterment. A necessary constituent of the genre is the form of a journey, undertaken to gather experience, and on which (under a certain selective theme) an instructive *revue* is being presented. Weise's contemporaries as well considered the journey an element necessary to the genre of the political novel. For example, the author of *Politische Mausefalle* [...] *Von Veritano Germanica* (1683) writes:

Es ist sonst in dergleichen Scriptis gebräuchlich, eine lustige Reise-Compagnie vorzustellen, die man mit gutem Rechte unter die Classe bringen könte, damit das Buch in dem Titel bezeichnet ist.[62]

It is otherwise in writings of this kind customary to introduce a happy company of travelers, which could rightfully be relegated to the class of people denoted by the title of the book.

Weise himself has made theoretical statements concerning the political novel, adding a sort of treatise on poetics of the genre in his *Kurtzer Bericht vom Politischen Näscher* (1680 and 1694), a kind of formula of how one should go about writing political novels according to a number of given rules. Here, just as in his preface to his *Erznarren*, Weise justifies his political novels by demonstrating their moral purpose. They should not contain attacks on specific individuals but only a general criticism of vice. In order to make the books attractive to the reader, he gives four formulas for engaging the emotions of the reader:

(1) Since the reader himself strives for the greatest possible degree of happiness on earth, the narrations must relate increasing success in business, honor, wealth, and love.

(2) In order to satisfy the reader's "curious" nature, extraordinary, "curious" things must be related.

(3) Since the reader considers only himself to be intelligent and probably also wishes to have something to criticize and correct, the writer must present to his judgment cases of folly, simplistic behavior, and so on.

(4) Since the reader desires to play the judge, he should be enabled to participate in reward or punishment for his own entertainment.

In addition, Weise makes suggestions for additional political novels by suggesting titles and by giving detailed advice for their writing; for example, he recommends a *Politischer Quacksalber*, a *Politischer Leyermann*, a *Politische Trödelfrau*, *Politisches Podagra*, *Politisches Zahnweh*, *Politisches Reißen im Leibe*, and other titles. It is understood that in this short work on poetics he also demands that the political novel communicate a certain number of wise and decent maxims for life.

This "report" fully served its purpose. It triggered the publication of a considerable number of political novels which, during the following decade, dominated the literature of Central Germany. It was primarily Johannes Riemer (1681-1714),[63] Weise's colleague and successor as professor of poetry and rhetoric at the *Gymnasium* in Weißenfels, who utilized the format of the political novel in works such as *Der Politische Maul-Affe* (1679), *Die Politische Colica* (1680), and *Der Politische Stock-Fisch* (1682), thereby achieving a new high point in this genre. In comparison to Weise he distinguishes himself, especially by his more natural narrative style, overcoming the abstract-didactic elements which are found in his predecessor's novels. Instead of artificially constructed individual scenes, he depicts atmospheric reality, he also adopts the bourgeois-political life goals, but in a more natural way. Even after Riemer's death the genre can be traced through the first decades of the eighteenth century.[64]

CHAPTER 3

The Courtly-Historical Novel

I *The* Amadis *novel*

PRECURSOR of the courtly-historical novel in Germany is the *Amadis* novel. Probably no German courtly-historical novel, regardless of whether it was written in a similar style or consciously in opposition to it, can deny that the *Amadis* novel was its ancestor. The *Amadis* novel originated in Spain around 1490, probably as an imitation of a Portuguese model. Originally comprising four volumes, the Spanish version had already been increased to twelve. A translation into French, begun in 1540, added nine additional volumes, drawing on Italian sources for the most part; and the German translation, which was published by Feyerabend in Frankfurt a.M. from 1569 to 1595, added three more, which were freely invented imitations, so that the entire novel now comprised twenty-four volumes altogether, with a total number of about twenty-five thousand pages in quarto format. The *Amadis* novel was so popular that it was republished in 1617, becoming one of the most popular discourses on noble society in the entire seventeenth century.

Its plot is generally the same as that of the medieval verse epics, slightly varied within the individual books, approximately according to the following scheme: A virtuous knight (Amadis himself or one of his sons) rides out in search of adventure; he fights against giants and dragons and wages fierce struggles against dwarfs and magicians. He frees imprisoned princesses who offer him their hand and crown; he, however, remains faithful to his lady, continuing to search for more adventures and new fame. His exploits are undertaken out of lust for adventure, without entailing ethical motivation or tragic conflicts. Numerous descriptions of tournaments, weapons, and styles of dress aid in re-creating the colorful splendor of a fairy-tale atmosphere. Fairies, magicians, griffins, and dragons are the elements of this world, and allegories embellish like arabesque ornaments.

97

However, what distinguishes these novels from the medieval epics is the fact that the system of knightly values is no longer intact. Not only do the knights engage in outright robbery and looting—the king no longer being powerful enough to punish them—they also no longer observe marital fidelity. The place of adoring love, the medieval *Minne,* has been taken by refined sensuality and obscenity. In many instances, the courtly ladies, driven by sensual love, take the initiative and pay nightly visits to their favorite knights. The spicy erotic scenes had increased in number, especially in the French translations, whereas the German redactions preferred to include moral considerations as well, thus offering the reader an excuse for perusing the more erotic parts. It was these erotic elements especially, which inspired Andreas Heinrich Buchholtz to compose his novels as consciously intended opposites to the *Amadis* novel. Although the German courtly-historical novels of the seventeenth century borrowed extensively from the *Amadis* novel, polemics against this work were carried on throughout the seventeenth century.[1]

II *The Courtly-Historical Novel: Foreign Influences and Genre Criteria*

The genre of the courtly-historical novel developed during the first half of the seventeenth century in France with authors such as Marin de Gomberville (*Polexandre* [1637], *Carithée* [1662]) becoming the great literary fashion during the 1640's and 1650's. Novels constituting many volumes were published, such as *Le Grand Cyre* (10 vols., 1649-53) and *Clélie* (10 vols., 1654-60), both written by Mlle de Scudéry, and *Cléopâtre* (12 vols., 1647-58) and *Cassandre* (10 vols., 1642-50), both written by the Seigneur de La Calprenède. The most important French novels were soon translated into German, thus affecting the literary taste in Germany for decades thereafter—i.e., before the great original German novels came into being.

Although Gomberville's *Carithée* had already been published in the first volume of a collection entitled *Theatrum Amoris* (1624), the actual stimulus for further translations came from Martin Opitz, who in 1626 published his translation of *Argenis* (Latin, 1621; French, 1623), a novel of state affairs which is also a romance. Its author was the Scotsman John Barclay (1582-

1621), who had become a French citizen. This translation by the influential organizer and initiator of German Baroque literature established the novel as a legitimate and recognized genre in Germany. In contrast to the *Amadis* novel, love and adventure remained in the background in *Argenis*, forming simply the frame on which political ideas were hung. An imaginary Sicilian state forms the basis for discussions on the absolute state of the seventeenth century. Recognized ethical standards emphasize the contrast with the *Amadis* novel.

Two years before this translation, in the fifth chapter of his epoch-making treatise on poetics, the *Buch von der Deutschen Poetery* (1624), Opitz had talked about the "heroic poem," that is, the epic, actually suggesting themes, style, and structure—one of the few observations in the critical writings of the seventeenth century which may be applied to the genre of the novel.

Translations and redactions of additional French novels appeared in rapid sequence: In 1644 G. A. Richter translated *Ariane* (1632) by Armand Desmaret, a protégé of the powerful French Cardinal Richelieu. During the same year, Philipp von Zesen published his translation of a novel by Vital d'Audiguier, entitled *Lysander und Caliste* (first version, 1616; second version, 1650). In 1645 Zesen produced a German translation of Mlle de Scudéry's *Ibrahim Bassa* (4 vols., 1641), and in 1647, *Afrikanische Sophonisbe*, originally by François du Soucy de Gerzan.[2] A *Verhochdeutschte Kleopatra* (La Calprenède) was published by the poet Georg Neumark in 1651, and in 1664 Johann Wilhelm von Stubenberg's translation of Mlle de Scudéry's *Clélie* appeared. La Calprenède's *Cassandre* was translated by Christian W. Hagdorn in 1670, and the German *Cleopatra* (translated by a certain J. V.) did not appear in complete form before 1700. In the meantime, the great German courtly-historical novels had been published, inspired by foreign models, nevertheless independent from them, expressing their own individuality and character.

In works of literary criticism, the term denoting the genre of the *höfisch-historischer Roman* ("courtly-historical novel") is changing, depending on which aspects or attributes of the genre the respective critics prefer to stress. Thus, besides the term here employed, which has been suggested by Günther Müller,[3] we find terms such as *heroischer Roman* ("heroic novel"),

höfischer Roman ("courtly novel") or even, following Opitz'
Argenis translation, *Staatsroman* ("novel of state affairs"). This
may be confusing because all these terms stand for more or less
the same literary phenomenon, especially since, during the seventeenth century, genre requirements (even in the form of unwritten
conventions) were far more rigid than they are today. The
present is a time in which *genre* has become a rather questionable term, the experiment of form being, for the most part, held
in higher esteem than the poet's obligation to *poetological*
norms. In the seventeenth century, the courtly-historical novel
(and this was the only type of novel which was recognized
by the numerous works on poetics) treated only certain specific
subjects; it used certain recurring repeated motifs, characters,
narrative techniques, a specific structure, a world view, a certain
message, as well as an appropriate language and style. In all
these points, the courtly-historical novel stands in sharp contrast to the picaresque novel; in many respects, it is its exact
opposite.[4]

The difference becomes obvious even in the social strata to
which the characters, the heroes and heroines belong. Whereas
the picaresque novel concentrated almost exclusively on the
lower classes, on rogues, thieves, soldiers, beggars, innkeepers,
and the like, the characters of the courtly-historical novels all
belong to a high, or the highest, social class: the main characters
are princes, princesses, and rulers of all ranks. In addition to
them we encounter noble courtiers, generals, high priests, and
possibly shepherds or hermits, who in most cases turn out to be
disguised princes. There are, of course, also servants and
soldiers, but the servants remain nameless, and the huge armies
are anonymous masses which are foils to the greatness and the
splendor of their ruler, being slaughtered by the hundreds of
thousands for the sake of one prince or princess. Since the hero
and the heroine are always of the ruling class, that is, princes
and princesses, love for them is no private affair, but rather
determines the fate of countries, crowns, or empires. Whereas
the wicked characters make war out of political considerations and reasons of state, the hero wages a war for ethical
reasons, as, for example, in order to free his beloved princess
from the hands of a wicked abductor. The high birth of the

hero and the heroine makes the courtly-historical novel at the same time a novel of state affairs.

The internal as well as external character traits correspond to the high social rank of both hero and heroine. As the hero is handsome, strong, and courageous, the heroine, too, has an almost superhuman beauty, intelligence, and amiability. The hero is able to put to flight entire armies almost single-handedly, while the bodies are being piled high around him. The heroine, too, may compete with her male counterpart in courage and heroism when the situation demands it. These esthetic qualities and heroic virtues are matched by ethical ones. Noble-mindedness and behavior according to generally accepted rules of good manners are expected traits. In addition, the hero and the heroine are characterized by virtues which originate in the scriptures of the Church Fathers and in Christian Stoicism. Integrity of character, open-mindedness and generosity, and harmony of the whole personality are termed *Großmut* ("magnanimity"). *Großmut* is accompanied by the second principal virtue, *Beständigkeit* ("constancy"), the equanimity which the heroes and heroines display in the face of all dangers and when they express their affections without ever doubting their love, rejecting all possible temptations of lust, wealth, and power. The love between hero and heroine is not sensual or lustful but is solely evidenced in admiration from a distance and a mutual worship, a kiss being considered almost sinful. Chastity is the ruling force of this love. The lovers shower one another with elaborate compliments, compose arias about the depth of their affection, poems, and letters of love for each other, continually assuring one another of their constancy. Thus, love is merely a touchstone of virtuous behavior; it is not a sensual, erotic experience, but an ethical element. In the feeling of love, the courtly-historical novel offers a field for the realization of virtue and thus of perfection within this world. The heroes are no individual persons in themselves, but rather types, embodiments of virtues, materializations of all social, ethical, and esthetic values of the time.

Often in these novels the hero is opposed by an antihero, a figure totally evil, as, for example, the tyrant Chaumigrem in Zigler's *Die Asiatische Banise*. In a reversal of the positive ideal of the hero, all courtly, ethical, and esthetic qualities the hero possesses are negated. The wicked antihero displays ugly features and often has a disproportionate figure; he is not courageous but cowardly; he does not observe the accepted code of behavior; and instead of generosity and magnanimity he displays extreme cruelty. Instead of virtues he displays desires and lusts such as arrogance and an unchecked sexual drive, lacking, of course, the virtue of constancy. Instead of self-discipline and self-restriction, he is characterized by a lack of chasteness and moderation. The antihero is thus the man who is dominated by affects and passions.

Corresponding to the high standing of the main characters are the objects described and the grand structures depicted, which always excel in size, beauty, and splendor. The setting receives the touch of the unusual by the writer's contrasting the world of the novel with the world of the reader in *two* ways: First, the action of the courtly-historical novels for the most part takes place in distant countries, ideally in the Middle East, or at least somewhere in the Mediterranean. Connected with this feature is the fact that the courtly-historical novel generally contains long journeys: the hero and the heroine are often separated from each other, and the entire known world has to be traversed before they can be reunited. Thus, the novel gives the reader the feeling of a geographical spaciousness. And when the novel, as it often happens, takes place in distant and exotic countries, there is an opportunity to describe exotic customs. Second, the setting is artificially rendered exotic since the action of the novel tends to take place in the historical past. Roman, Egyptian, Indic, biblical, and Germanic antiquity are the most popular epochs of history.

The novelist takes pain to describe the background of time and place as realistically as possible. Therefore, the facts are in most cases correct, because before composing his work, the author has carefully studied the historical and geographical sources, consulting an entire array of historiographies and/or travelogues. The same characteristic applies to insertions of cultural history which may take up many pages; these were based on articles of the great popular encyclopedic cultural-historical collections of the time. The sources are often either directly quoted in the running text as footnotes, or they are appended to the novels, at times, with lengthy quotations in numerous languages, for example, in Zesen's *Assenat*. As previously noted, the seventeenth century did not operate under modern coypright laws, so that often whole pages were literally copied or translated from the sources. The novelist inserts his numerous historical or cultural essays for several reasons. On the one hand, he can demonstrate his own knowledge and learning, for a poet was still considered to be a scholar in addition to being a writer. The communication of knowledge lends his work dignity, and, by its simultaneous presence, he justifies the fictional contents of the work. On the other hand, the novelist met a genuine demand on the part of the reader, who demanded to be presented encyclopedic knowledge and for whom Eichendorff's famous characterization of courtly-historical novels as *tollgewordene Realenzyklopädien* ("mad encyclopedias") would have actually been a compliment to the genre. The seventeenth century may rightfully be called the encyclopedic century because such knowledge enjoyed high esteem. Evidences of this are the tedious compilations, which novelists utilized for their works; curiosities of a scientific, historical, folkloristic nature; the so-called prodigy literature, which listed all kinds of strange facts and unusual happenings, such as the birth of monsters and the appearances of comets; and travelogues, in which true and fantastic stories were recounted side by side.

However, courtly-historical novels were not only encyclopedias. At the same time, they were compendia for correct moral and social behavior: in place of insertions which serve to communicate factual, encyclopedic knowledge, we often find elaborate moralistic and theological excursions. Moralistic maxims and general truths are, in many cases, stressed by the technique of printing them in bold-faced type. In the case of Daniel Casper von Lohenstein's *Arminius*, these maxims and moralistic insertions were, at a later period, considered so important that they were published separately as a collection of moralistic homilies.[5] Numerous inserted letters and models of complimenting—according to the standards of etiquette of the day—served to render the works models for exemplary behavior, a tendency in the literature which was to reach its high point with the gallant novel at the end of the seventeenth century. In brief, the courtly-historical novels were not only entertaining by reason of their plot, but they were at the same time edifying and instructive. They communicated knowledge of the most diverse kind—whatever the author considered adequate and appropriate for his prospective reading public. The static insertions, entailing descriptions of objects, customs, and moralistic excursions produced, with regard to narrative technique, a suspension of time, since the continuum of action is continually interrupted. However, by suspending the temporal dimension, these insertions fulfill the need to stress the spatial dimension of the courtly-historical novel; this is also achieved by recounting the characters' various journeys and travels.

From its beginnings in France, the courtly-historical novel is in practically all cases also a *roman à clef*, a *Schlüsselroman*. This means that the plot of the novel becomes *transparent*, in that the frequently genuine historical figures often represent completely different characters of the author's seventeenth-century day. Thus, the courtly-historical novel may become a political analogy or an indirect account of the family history of the European principalities. Recognizing just what and who was concealed behind the exterior façade most definitely contributed to the enjoyment of reading, although the disguise was often very skillfully applied. In fact, the individual character could represent different contemporary or historical persons within the novel (Lohenstein's *Arminius*). Other authors took a factual event of their own time simply as a poetic subject, as an interesting story, without the intention of making it into a puzzle, something to be deciphered by the reader (Duke Anton Ulrich).

The world of the courtly-historical novel appears, at first glance, to be a fatalistic, gruesome, and confusing one. The lives of its characters are dominated by *Fortuna*, the allegorical figure of the world, whose eternal vacillation is symbolized by a wheel. She is responsible for the incessant changing of the characters' fates. Yet the protagonists prove their merits, in spite of the dominance of *Fortuna*, through the virtue of constancy, thereby evading the power of the goddess. Even if their bodies cannot always resist, their spirits and their minds can. Whereas the *picaro* succumbs to the world, becoming trapped by its vices, and comes to himself—if at all—only at the end, the heroes of the courtly-historical novel continue their resistance successfully. They are able to steadfastly maintain their identity and the integrity of their own selves. In contrast to the situation encountered in the picaresque novel, their endeavors are, there-fore, more in the nature of a passive affirmation of their virtuous-ness against the attacks of the capricious goddess than a real, active struggle in a hand-to-hand fight for survival. In this passive resistance, reliance on their constancy is not a simple trusting in a personal virtue, but rather the hero and heroine's belief in the final solution of the struggle in their favor, because they believe in the final victory of Divine Providence over *Fortuna,* a concept which is termed *die Vorsehung Gottes, die Vorsehung der Götter,* or simply *der Himmel.* Thus, in the final apotheosis of the united couples, Divine Providence is victorious; indeed, it becomes obvious that the entire confusing nature of the novel's plot was not in the least arbitrary or haphazard, but rather that Divine Providence was constantly guarding and protecting its protégés, finally securing their eternal happiness. Whereas the world often appeared in the eyes of the characters of the novel as one dominated by terrifying confusion and in those of the reader as a beautifully constructed labyrinth, the "happy ending" makes it very clear that the action had functioned with the precision of a clock in accordance with the preconceived plan of Divine Providence. When the protagonists finally receive the just reward for their virtuous behavior, their virtuousness is ultimately realized in an external system of order as well, and the world is inwardly as well as outwardly "safe and sound."

The structure of the courtly-historical novel follows a principle which was popular in the novels, written in the "high" style, since the time of the late Greek *Ethiopiea* by Heliodorus,[6] the principle being, namely, that of unification—separation—re-unification, which can best be illustrated graphically (p. 106): At the beginning of the novel, or at least during the first part of the work, the hero falls in love with the heroine—but their ultimate union is delayed by all sorts of obstacles. War breaks out, or the heroine is abducted—in one way or another, the two are geographically separated from each other. The hero carries on his search for the heroine throughout the entire known world. She, in the meantime, is threatened by her abductor, or by the usurper of the throne, with marriage—if necessary by force—or more simply her chastity may be endangered. In many instances she can save herself only by means of her amazingly heroic qualities, perhaps even by killing the villain. The hero,

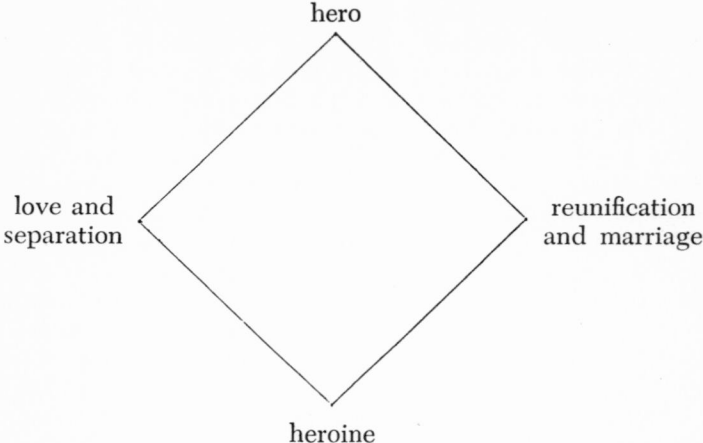

too, is endangered; beautiful women attempt to entangle him in their scheming nets, princesses offer their love to him, robbers obstruct his way, and attempts on his life are made until at the conclusion, in spite of all difficulties thus far encountered, the couple is finally united in wedlock. The courtly-historical novel ends in a celebration, with marriage and the security of a throne. A seemingly eternal order has prevailed.

In most cases, the main plot is, to a certain degree, duplicated and echoed by subplots, supporting actions which serve to mirror the main action: the hero has friends and companions; the heroine, confidantes or servants. Thus, several stories which follow the same structural scheme are connected with each other, or run parallel to one another, all concurring at the end. Duke Anton Ulrich's novels have as many as thirty-four couples, a number of them bearing identical names, and Andreas Heinrich Buchholtz' novels number up to 450 characters, so that the reader is compelled to devise for himself indices and genealogical charts if he wants to fully understand and follow the entire action.

The situation is further complicated by the fact that imposture, deception, and intrigue are the novel's main ingredients: The identity of persons becomes confused because two or more characters are referred to by the same name; they disguise themselves on purpose, take on other, borrowed names; or they conceal their identities by pretending to be of their opposite sex, which becomes especially interesting in the case of marriages with a change of sex on the part of both characters. Numerous intrigues are initiated by the dispatch of forged letters or deliberate delivery of the right ones to the wrong individual. The hero or the heroine is often believed to be dead, but is actually still alive, and so on. The entire novel is thus characterized by an atmosphere of considerable intrigue and deception.

Besides the continually recurring motifs of deception, there are additional ones, which are also repeated over and over again; there are robbers who bar the hero's way, whom he must kill in order to prove his bravery; and there are pirates who abduct the princess, threaten her chastity, and carry her off to distant countries. Many of these motifs—for example, the motifs of disguise, the shipwrecks, storms at sea, attempts at blackmail, seduction, abduction, expulsion, or the appearance of pirates—can be traced in literary history as far back as the Hellenistic novels. Thus, the stereotyped structural principle and the uniformity of the ethos are supplemented by a whole series of certain individual motifs, which the author inserts into the novel just as if he were fitting mechanical parts into a machine.

The narrative technique as well is of late Greek origin, which contributes considerably to systematically confusing the reader, as most courtly-historical novels do not narrate the events in the natural sequence of time (the order in which the events actually took place), but, instead, become directly involved in the center of the action. Actually, the action has reached its first high point well before the beginning of the novel since, at the start, the protagonists are already involved in a situation from which there does not seem to be any way out, and they loudly lament their adverse fate, attributing it to the whims of fortune. The best example of this *in medias res* technique is probably Heinrich Anshelm von Zigler und Kliphausen's *Die Asiatische Banise*, the beginning of which will be quoted below. The beginning of the novel makes it necessary to reveal the events leading up to the present as well as to indicate those to come, in order to bring the reader up to date. This is done, in most cases, by having one of the main characters recount his story. As new characters are introduced, their biographies, too, are related, so that the reader is continually kept up with the state of affairs at the time in which the story is related, that is, with the narrative present. Into these narrations, in turn, other narrations may be inserted. However, all narrations may be interrupted by the events of the action of the narrative present, so that the biographies cannot be completed until at a much later point in the work.

Whereas the main action—in contrast to the picaresque novel— is supplied by the anonymous author, the inserted biographies are told by the respective characters themselves. The fact that at least one main *couple* is being dealt with requires, furthermore, a separate report of their adventure sequences. This is not done by first relating the adventures of the hero and, following that, those of the heroine. Instead, both are reported "simultaneously," by first relating a bit of action A (hero), then a bit of action B (heroine), and so on, so that an alternating narrative sequence results. Thus, from the very outset, the narrative technique produces an artificial state of confusion which can be said to resemble the intricate paths and byways of the seventeenth-century gardens!

As all these generic criteria demonstrate, the courtly-historical novel is, in comparison to the pastoral and the picaresque novel, an extremely complex and artistically constructed type of literature, which, strikingly, mirrors the spirit of the courtly seventeenth century. Its existence is fundamentally based on the existence of the courtly culture which formed the basis of cultural life in Germany. This dependence of the genre on certain social conditions resulted in the fact that this type of the novel was able to stay alive only for a relatively short period of time. In its unadulterated form, with strict adherence to its inner ethos, it was in existence only until about 1690, when it was replaced by the lighter, more frivolous gallant novel, which, in turn, was fostered by the emergence of a new, less dramatic society, with a new philosophy of life.

III *Andreas Heinrich Buchholtz:* Herkules und Valiska;
Herkuliskus und Herkuladisla

Andreas Heinrich Buchholtz was born on November 25, 1607, in Schöningen, in the vicinity of Halberstadt. He studied theology in Wittenberg and Rostock, was a teacher in Hameln and in Lemgo, and in 1641 became a professor of practical philosophy and poetry, and later of theology as well, in Rinteln. In 1647 he became a high official in the church administration at Braunschweig, where in 1664 he was appointed superintendent of all churches in the city, and school inspector. He died on May 20, 1671, in Braunschweig.

Buchholtz wrote two voluminous novels: *Des Christlichen Teutschen Groß-Fürsten Herkules und der Böhmischen Königlichen Fräulein Valiska Wunder-Geschichte* (two parts, Braunschweig, 1659/60) and a sequel, *Der Christlichen Königlichen Fürsten Herkuliskus und Herkuladisla auch Ihrer Hochfürstlichen Gesellschaft anmuthige Wunder-Geschichte* (Braunschweig, 1665).[7]

In *Herkules und Valiska* the German prince Herkules is abducted and sold as a slave in Rome, where he converts to Christianity. His friend, the Bohemian prince Ladisla, frees him and marries Sophia, the daughter of the Roman governor of Padua. Herkules' fiancée, the Bohemian princess Valiska, is kidnapped on her journey to the wedding. Following this is the pursuit of the kidnappers into the Middle East, Valiska's chastity being threatened by prurient Oriental rulers, and the consolidation of the main characters' reign after the heroes have freed Valiska and have returned to Germany.

In *Herkuliskus und Herkuladisla*, the two title figures, the sons of the two primary couples of the first novel, travel to the Middle East in order to bring their aunt Clara, a grand duchess in Persia, home with them. They succeed in doing this only after all sorts of dangerous encounters and battles, and at the end they each marry the sister of the other.

The number of characters in both novels is extremely high, so that Buchholtz has included in the second novel an index of the characters, which lists over 450 names. The reader of modern works of literature can only surmise how complicated and confused the action gets because of identical names, change of names, sex, and so on.

According to the preface of *Herkuliskus*, both novels were written during the 1640's, the work on *Herkuliskus* having been started soon after Buchholtz completed his work on *Herkules*. According to his own pronouncement, the author wanted to establish the genre of a German courtly-historical novel, which, in contrast to the *Amadis* novel, is supposed to be moralistic and realistic. Two tendencies in the *Amadis* novel especially annoyed the theologian Buchholtz: on the one hand, the numerous lascivious and obscene stories, which contributed to the popularity of the novel, especially among young people; and, on the other hand, the stories about ghosts, magic, and miracles, of which the *Amadis* novel boasted an equal number. In other words, with his novels, Buchholtz wanted to counteract the corrupting and demoralizing aspects of the *Amadis* novel. For that reason, in his two sequential novels, there are no sorcerers and witches, no tribes of giants, and no fabulous or legendary animals. His heroes' numerous adventures are by far more reasonably motivated than in the *Amadis* novel: they do not, like the *Amadis* knights, ride out in search of adventures, but either in order to educate themselves through travel or to free their beloved girl from the hands of her abductors. Buchholtz, to be sure, does use numerous motifs already employed in the *Amadis* novel and in the knightly chapbooks; however, he selects according to the principles of probability and moral utility.

Buchholtz' didactic intent is the propagation of a Christian moral through the novel. As he wants to assign new values to the seductive pastime of the *Amadis* novel, he invests it with a new message. In contrast to the latter there are, for example, no numerous pre- or extramarital love adventures. In any case, Buchholtz' hero marries his lady before approaching her physically. Thus, Herkules and Valiska marry by praying and joining hands, since the possibility of getting a priest does not exist. Because of this moralistic attitude the number of marriages in both novels is extremely high, and Buchholtz preaches with ardent zeal against love relationships which are established without parents' knowledge. The consent of parents or their representatives must always be secured before each marriage. Thus, the author advocates the etiquette of the seventeenth century by utilizing characters out of the third century. In the event that, at the time of the wedding, one member of the couple is still heathen, the other uses the opportunity to save the soul of his beloved by converting him or her to Christianity.

Buchholtz' heroes are characterized stereotypically either as archvillains or as faultless heroes and heroines. There is no trace of a psychological discrimination of individual characters or a moral distinction, as, for example, Duke Anton Ulrich was trying to achieve. All morally good characters are either Christians or are converted to Christianity during the course of the novel. If a Christian and a heathen fight each other, this fight is considered an ordeal, and the Christian is bound to win, because God is on his side. This religious emphasis, which is somewhat naïve and one-sided, is brought out not only by the insertion of numerous prayers, pious songs, and psalms but especially by extensive "heathen conversions." Again and again the heathens are confronted with the excellence of the Christian religion and ethic, and submission to God's will is preached above all. Man is not supposed to rebel against his fate, no matter how difficult it may be for him to carry on, because God will bring everything to a successful end. The good are rewarded, and the wicked receive their well-deserved punishment. Everything has its inherent logic and turns out for the best. The Braunschweig superintendent defends the entire order of the world as moral and Christian from the standpoint of the Christian doctrine of faith. The general tenor of his novels is religious pathos.

The action of both novels, to be sure, takes place during the third century, but, exactly as in Zigler's *Die Asiatische Banise,* the heroes show traits of seventeenth-century figures. Herkules is a hero like those of the Thirty Years' War; his appearance and his behavior are those of an ostentatious theatrical hero. Along with this must be considered the fact that, in contrast to other authors of courtly-historical novels, Buchholtz offers his reader hardly any historical or local color. The early Germans, for example, are drawn with a few rough lines, based on sketchy reports of Caesar and Tacitus. The German archduke Heinrich, Herkules' father, is residing—in the third century A.D.(!)—in a huge castle. He presides over splendid courtly festivities and dubs many worthy youths knights. The Bohemians are described in a similarly anachronistic fashion: Ladisla and Valiska are brought up believing in the gods and goddesses of classical antiquity; a native Bohemian religion is not even mentioned. In Europe as well as in Asia the reader encounters a medieval knightly culture—even Jewish knights appear—which totally erases national differences.

Buchholtz does not indulge in Orientalisms, exotic customs,

or the like. In this connection, it is typical that he does not name the sources he has consulted.

A strongly patriotic tendency is expressed in the brief but heroic description of the Germans and Bohemians, a tendency which will be found to be even more pronounced in Lohenstein's *Arminius*. For example, the armies of the Middle Eastern tyrants can be defeated only by the bravery of the German and Bohemian contingents. In the friendship between Germans and Bohemians, the revival of the old idea of a *Reich,* which the author is, therefore, seen to be advocating, is observable. Without doubt, he is attempting to ennoble his novels and to stimulate the patriotism of the Germans by selecting plots taken from German history and legends.

Instead of local and historical color or endless descriptions of customs, an enormous number of inserted discussions and essays of all kinds are found. Psalms and prayers are supplemented by numerous theological discussions, entire sermons, and disputations. Many areas of subject matter are discussed: human existence, the nature and omnipotence of God, the *summum bonum,* the oath, various heretics and their fake doctrines, and the like. Besides such theological subjects there are essays on historical, astronomical, literary, and philosophical themes. The princes are instructed on ways to govern their peoples wisely; the founding and the development of the various cities are mentioned.

Buchholtz' novels are composed entirely in the fashion of the courtly-historical novel. The author starts *in medias res*; he then relates the prelude to the story. He narrates, piece by piece, the various life histories of the novels' characters, fitting their fate into the Heliodoric scheme and holding off the reunification of the separated lovers by introducing ever new "retarding" elements. However, the works are distinguished from other courtly-historical novels by their emphatically Christian-moralistic spirit. On the one hand, the fact that the heroes embody Christian virtues, and, on the other, that directing the world behind the scenes there is not an anonymous *Verhängnis* ("fate") or just *der Himmel* ("heaven") but the Christian God, who guarantees a happy outcome to man's fate.

The style, indeed the entire manner of presentation in both novels, is rather dry and lifeless. The overemphasis placed on the religious and the moralistic-didactic definitely contributes to this shortcoming. Lively, vivid description can be found only in the narration of the love between Herkules and Valiska and of the friendship between Herkules and Ladisla. The vividness achieved by these, however, is missing in the second novel, which, on this level, has little more to offer than numerous themes and much action. Compared with Buchholtz' first novel, its artistic value is considerably lower.

The importance of Buchholtz' two novels in literary history lies in the fact that they terminated the exclusively dominant position of the *Amadis* novel in Germany as being the only novel written in a "high" style set within the upper classes of society. They introduce the genre of the courtly-historical novel into Germany, which at this time already enjoyed considerable popularity abroad.

IV *Herzog Anton-Ulrich von Braunschweig-Wolffenbüttel*:
Aramena *and* Octavia

The most outstanding examples of the German Baroque novel were produced by a ruling duke. Between 1669 and 1673 Duke Anton Ulrich von Braunschweig-Wolffenbüttel's first mammoth work appeared, *Die Durchleuchtige Syrerinn Aramena,* in five volumes comprising almost four thousand pages. Between 1677 and 1707 an even more voluminous novel was published—*Octavia, Römische Geschichte* in six volumes comprising almost seven thousand pages in quarto format, which in 1712 was republished under the title *Die Römische Octavia.*

Duke Anton Ulrich was born on October 4, 1633, in the little town of Hitzacker in the province of Lüneburg. He was given a very thorough education, with special emphasis on the liberal arts. Among his teachers were the poets and literary theoreticians; Justus August Schottel (1612-76); and, for a period, Siegmund von Birken (1626-81). The duke's education was rounded out by studies in Helmstedt and extended trips through Germany, France, and Italy. In 1704 Anton Ulrich succeeded his brother August as the ruler of the duchy. Since Rudolf August had no male heirs, he made Anton Ulrich his co-regent in 1685. In 1710 Anton Ulrich secretly converted to Catholicism, probably in a futile attempt to acquire the bishopric of Mayence. He died on March 27, 1714, in his castle, Salzdahlum. Anton Ulrich, a politically energetic Baroque prince with a distinct love for power and splendor, started out as a poet by writing Lutheran church songs, religious odes, and a number of dramatic *Singspiele* for courtly festivities, utilizing biblical themes and motifs from German history. His two novels doubtlessly represent his greatest literary achievement.

The action of *Die Durchleuchtige Syrerinn Aramena* takes place in the biblical age of Jacob and centers around the heroic couple, Aramena and Cimber (Marsius). Over a long period of time, the two lovers must endure numerous threats and tricks, for they are persecuted by a tyrant before they are united, and they rule Germany from the city of Treves.

Octavia, the heroine of the duke's second novel, was married as a child to the Roman emperor Nero, who, however, repudiates her. When he orders her executed and proceeds to carry out this threat, she is saved at the last moment by the nobel Tyridates, King of Armenia. But before the two can be united, Tyridates has to prove himself by fighting his brothers, while in the meantime law and order are reinstated in the Roman Empire by Emperor Vespasian. Over and over again, Octavia must prove her virtue and Tyridates his constancy; both of them succeed because of their firm belief in Christianity.

By comparing the original manuscripts, Blake Lee Spahr has demonstrated that a preliminary, shorter version of *Aramena* was probably written by Sybille Ursula, a sister of the duke.[8] The duke himself then supplied the more detailed version, the amplification and the stylistic changes, whereas the poet Siegmund von Birken took charge of the final editing and stylistic reworking and supervised the printing.

The joint enterprise is, however, not restricted to this collaboration. Spahr was able to prove that numerous appended and inserted poems of the novel as well as the pastoral play "Schäferspiel von Jacob / Lea und Rahel" (vol. V, pp. 461-86) were not written by Anton Ulrich but by Siegmund von Birken. The poetess Catharina Regina von Greiffenberg (1633-94) has also been credited with contributing numerous poems. To her, the "Unbekannte Freundin" ("unknown friend"), the fifth volume of *Aramena* is dedicated. Again, it would be a mistake to apply the modern concept of copyright to a Baroque novel.

In this particular case, Anton Ulrich's high social rank has to be taken into consideration above all. The authors of the poems which had become part of this monumental novel felt honored rather than cheated, as is evident from a remark by Catharina Regina von Greiffenberg.[9]

Anton Ulrich's novels are, to a certain extent, *romans à clef*, a characteristic which immediately leads to a discussion of their genre affiliation. The fifth volume of *Aramena* bears the title "Mesopotamische Schäferei." Here the characters involved in the main action engage in a kind of masked ball, disguising as shepherds, who, in contrast to the real shepherds, distinguish themselves by their magnificent appearance and by their songs and arias. In short, here we have a pastoral novel of the type exemplified by Opitz' *Schäfferey* or Harsdörffer/Klaj's *Pegnesisches Schäfergedicht*— a social pastoral novel. Correspondingly the shepherds who sing and compose poetry represent not only the characters responsible for the main action but also living individuals of the seventeenth century, poets and poetesses who actually wrote those poems and arias. Thus, in Anton Ulrich's "Mesopotamische Schäferei," Ausicles is Anton Ulrich himself; Suriane, Sybille Ursula, his sister; Belisar, Siegmund von Birken; Uriane, Catharina Regina von Greiffenberg; Gerontas, Count Gottlieb von Windischgrätz; Sarung, Salzdahlum; Samosata, Saxony; and so on.[10] The fast-moving plot is slowed down for a period, as the work is temporarily transformed into a pastoral novel.

Most of the events of the action proper will hardly ever be identified with actual happenings. If Anton Ulrich did actually use intimate stories, family events, or scandalous gossip of the European courts, he most likely did so to stimulate his own fantasy, certainly not to write an identifiable and rather obvious key novel. Critics persist in suspecting that behind the novel action lay the reality of the seventeenth century, but without being able to produce a key which remains undisputed. An unequivocal decoding has been achieved in only one episode of *Octavia*, that of the Princess Solane in the sixth volume. Solane has been identified as Princess Sophia Dorothea, wife of Georg Ludwig, the crown prince of the electorate of Hanover, who later was to become George I, King of England. Sophia Dorothea allegedly had an affair with a certain Count Philipp

Christoph von Königsmarck. On the night of July 1, 1694, Königsmarck disappeared under mysterious circumstances in the Hanover castle. Most likely he was assassinated, and Sophia Dorothea was banned to a lonely dwelling in Ahlden for the rest of her life.[11] If Anton Ulrich also utilized other historical events, he must have disguised them so well or altered them so drastically that they are not identifiable, either for his contemporaries or for the modern reader. Thus the difference from the intended ambiguity of plot and characters in Lohenstein's *Arminius* is quite obvious.

In many respects, Anton Ulrich's novels represent the high point of the courtly-historical novel in Germany. This is especially true with regard to the intricate structure of the work in its entirety. Whereas the Hellenistic novel had, in most cases, only one story relating events which had taken place previous to the beginning of the novel, Anton Ulrich's novels encompass an endless number of these narrations, for his novel contains a great number of characters. In *Aramena* no less than thirty couples struggle for their final unification, achieving their goal in two great mass weddings which terminate the fourth and fifth volume.[12] Each of the two groups is headed by a couple of especially high social rank: the first one by Aramenes, the King of Syria, with Cœlidiane, the daughter of King Melchisedech of Salem; the other by Marsius, the King of the Germans, with Aramena, the sister of Aramenes. Beginning with these couples at the top of the social scale, there are gradations in rank all the way down to the simple shepherd couple. The fates of these couples are inextricably interwoven with the other ones. Each couple brings its own tale of previous events to the novel, the narrative being interrupted by the events of the narrative present, so that it must be continued at a later point. Thus, *Aramena* contains thirty narrations of previous happenings, the narration of which extends through the last volume. Of the approximately three hundred important characters of the novel about two hundred and fifty are relatives of some sort; the reader can hardly find his way through this "family jungle" without the aid of detailed genealogical tables. Such an enormous number of characters obviously requires an unparalleled ability in the art of characterization; the duke possessed this ability to a far greater degree than, for example, Buchholtz, who also deals with a like number of characters. This great number of characters makes it necessary, above all, to plan the structure of the whole very carefully, so that the entire work is presented to the reader as a giant puzzle; indeed, it appears to the characters themselves as a labyrinth affording no way out. In addition to this, both characters and readers are purposely confounded by the author. Numerous intended and unintended deceptions, misunderstandings, intrigues, disguises, and mixups of all sorts contribute to the general confusion. In *Aramena,* for example, there are thirty-five situations in which a character who was believed dead suddenly reappears; there are thirty cases in which a person is not the one whom others, or even he himself, considered him to be. Three marriages take place which are ultimately revealed to have only been a masquerade. One of the heroes, believed to be a descendant of Roman emperors, turns out to be a Germanic prince. The Canaanite prince Abimelech, the faithful lover of Delbois, learns at the peak of the personal and political confusion that he is actually the Syrian prince Aramenes and his loved one is his own sister Aramena.[13] Thus, the duke's novels—the situation in *Octavia* is quite similar—constitute an artificially created general confusion and its gradual disentanglement, primarily accomplished by the relating of the previous events and the resulting clarification of the true state of affairs: the individuals' fates are viewed from different standpoints, that is, from those of various narrations of antecedent events. In this way, a chain of cause and effect becomes apparent, which, up to the point of the narration of the individual story, remains hidden.[14] In this connection, critics have rightfully quoted a letter which the philosopher Gottfried Wilhelm Leibniz (1646-1716) wrote to Anton Ulrich from Vienna on April 26, 1713:

Es ist ohne dem eine von der Roman-Macher besten Künsten, alles in verwirrung fallen zu laßen, und dann unverhofft heraus zu wickeln.[15]

It is, in any event, one of the greatest skills of the novelists to create utter confusion, and then unexpectedly disentangle it.

This general confusion, and the numerous deceits and self-deceptions, are due to the fact that in the philosophy of life expressed in Anton Ulrich's novels there are three levels of reality:[16] (1) the objective world of the novel; the actual state of affairs

which is concealed to man as a whole; (2) the world of appearances, the world in which man lives, that is, a world of illusion.
Man is helpless in this world because he cannot distinguish
between truth and illusion; (3) the world of action, the fictional
world created by the will of man himself, because he cannot
distinguish between the objective world and the world of appearances. The actual state of affairs is, in the main, concealed from
the view of man, of the characters of the novel, as well as of the
reader. From time to time the veil is lifted slightly, and a bit
of reality is revealed—a process which is accomplished by the
narration of the preceding events. This "actual" reality represents, in its absolute truthfulness, the Divine order, the world
which is ruled by Divine Providence. However, man sees only
the second world, that of appearances. This is the form in which
reality is presented to him. Man is cheated and deceived by
the façade, since this is only a part of what is real. The decep-
tive appearances, leading to wrong assumptions, misdirect the
characters of the novel as well as the reader into wrong judgments and conclusions. Man attempts to discover the truth and
acts accordingly; he attempts to achieve his goal by disguising
or by altering his identity and deceives others in order to protect
himself, but he is, in turn, deceived. Thus, the human will
intervenes between the world of appearances and the world of
actions. In spite of this confusion, it is not impossible that,
ironically, man acts according to the world of appearances or
according to his will, and nevertheless according to reality, for
the world of appearances and that of reality, or the world of
actions and that of reality, may be identical. Thus, man unconsciously acts correctly, in spite of having been deceived, in
spite of his wrong judgments, and although he is still unable to
glimpse the true state of affairs.

A soothsayer prophesies that Dison will marry Aramena. That
is considered impossible by all, for everyone knows that both are
disguised. Dison is in reality Aramena, and Aramena is Dison!
The reader as well is deceived although he is conscious of *both*
true identities, because he misinterprets the soothsayer's prophesy
as irony. Dison and Aramena agree to a pretended marriage because they do not know each other's identity. But the reader
is deceived as well, in that the two really fall in love, and the
marriage takes place.[17]

Although man cannot witness reality, and although he is constantly in a state of deception, the order of the world proves to be a good one, as everything leads to that which is best for man, since reality is, in the end, ruled by Divine Providence directing everything toward a beneficial outcome, despite the general confusion. Thus, a fundamentally optimistic order of the world is presented. The entire novel presents a gradual progression toward the realization of the true state. Correspondingly, evil persons are punished in *this* world and the good rewarded, since if reality is identical with the Divine Order there can be no imbalance or injustice. Thus, Anton Ulrich's novels, representative of the German courtly-historical novel as such, describe the path from deception to insight to true reality. Whereas at first the goddess Fortune, who leads man through deceit and misery, appears to rule, in the final analysis Providence proves to be in command, rewarding constancy and love.

Essayistic insertions are not lacking in Anton Ulrich's novels; they are primarily of a political nature, as the duke's novels at the same time were intended to be *Fürstenspiegel*. The ideal is the benevolent, just, and virtuous ruler, who is contrasted with the tyrant. It is only fitting that a ruling duke should treat such a topic.

Correspondingly, the two works can not be considered historical novels. They contain even fewer historical facts than Lohenstein's *Arminius,* and history lends them little more than the place of action and the names of the characters. In *Aramena* Jacob and his women remain totally in the background, whereas all of the minor kings of the Middle East are raised in status. The characters in both novels do not display any characteristic of those of biblical antiquity. They behave just like cavaliers and ladies at the seventeenth-century European courts. The behavior of the characters is exemplary; they are meant to serve as models for the seventeenth-century reader. Thus, the duke's novels developed into model books of gentlemanlike behavior for the German nobility; his works are extremely rich in model conversations and letters, in which the characters seem to be competing in their displays of courtesy. What is missing are the great speeches, composed according to the rhetorical rules of the time, which are found in Buchholtz' and Zigler's novels. Equally absent are the scholarly insertions, which are characteristic of most of the other courtly-historical novels. In addition, we have no obtrusive moralistic, didactic elements. The courtly characters simply serve as models.

In *Aramena*,[18] religion still plays a relatively unimportant role. The most distinguished characters turn away from idolatry, focusing on the monotheism of the Old Testament, a conversion which is displayed as a positive change in their personalities. Aramena herself does not rest before her beloved Cimber and all of her friends have converted to her faith. Three powerful heathen temples—the temple of Diana in Niniveh, the temple of Isis in Damascus, and the temple of the Mesopotamian god Teraphim—are burned to the ground. *Octavia*,[19] however, takes place in early Christian times, and one of the themes is the diffusion and dissemination of Christian religion and the fate of the early Christians. The Christians are persecuted by the rulers and try, in turn, to influence the affairs of the state. Here, as well as in *Aramena,* the main emphasis is not placed on the pronouncement of strict religious dogmas; rather, the young faith is characterized as a new human attitude. In difficult and controversial points regarding religious particularities, the characters of the novel attempt to take a conciliatory position[20] (just as the duke himself was concerned about a reconciliation of the different denominations). In *Octavia* the death of the Apostles Paul, Peter, and Matthew is noted, and life in the catacombs of Rome and other cities is described. These particular descriptive passages seem to have made a marked impression upon Goethe, for he has his friend Susanna von Klettenberg refer to them in "Bekenntnisse einer schönen Seele" ("Confessions of a Beautiful Soul").[21]

Richard Alewyn has estimated that a reader would have to spend twelve hours a day for six weeks in order to read *Römische Octavia* and that his trouble would hardly be rewarded by the pleasure one would expect from a modern novel.[22] It seems, therefore, to be certain that, despite the availability of reprints of both novels, which are in the planning stage at the time of this writing, they will hardly be read by more than a few scholars in the field. But this fact does not detract from their importance for German literary history. Despite their length, their endless descriptions, complications and entanglements, they were the joy of their contemporaries and represented the highest achievement of the courtly-historical novel in Germany.

V *Daniel Casper von Lohenstein*: Arminius und Thusnelda

Highly praised during the seventeenth century as a stylistic model, but disdained during the eighteenth as an example of bombastic style was Daniel Casper von Lohenstein's novel, published posthumously in 1689/90 in two volumes in quarto format, and comprising altogether 3,076 pages: *Großmüthiger Feldherr Arminius oder Hermann [. . .] nebst seiner durchlauchtigen Thußnelda in einer sinnreichen Staats=, Liebes= und Helden= Geschichte*. This novel, the second volume of which was completed by Lohenstein's brother in collaboration with a preacher by the name of Wagner, was first published by the poet Benjamin Neukirch (1665-1729). It appeared in only one further edition (1731).

Lohenstein, whose original name was actually Daniel Casper, was born on January 25, 1635, in Nimptsch in Silesia. He attended the *Gymnasium* in Breslau and from 1651 on studied law in Leipzig and Tübingen, where in 1655 he was awarded the doctorate. An educational tour took him through Germany, Holland, Switzerland, and Austria. Following this, Lohenstein had an amazing career as a high-ranking official and diplomat, first holding the position of a government official in Oels (1665), then of a syndic in Breslau (1670), and finally of an emissary and imperial councilor (1675). He died on April 28, 1683, in Breslau. His fame as a poet is based not only on his authorship of *Arminius* but also on his six dramas, the setting of which is Roman and Egyptian-African antiquity and contemporary Turkey. Next to Andreas Gryphius (1616-64), Lohenstein is considered the greatest German dramatist of the Baroque period.

The plot of *Arminius* comes to mind with the name of the historical title hero: The biography of Arminius; his marriage and separation from Thusnelda; his struggle against the Romans; his betrayal by his own relatives, especially by Segestes, his father-in-law; the fate of his brother Flavius; and Roman politics with regard to Germany, as carried out by Roman leaders such as Augustus, Germanicus, Varus, and Tiberius. His relationship with Thusnelda, including their separation, constitutes the love action, which is mirrored in several parallel subplots. Arminius proves to be the prototype of the Baroque hero, who patiently accepts the blows of fate which rules the world created in the novel.

A comprehensive appendix of factual notes accompanies the novel, which, in this case, was compiled by its editors. Lohenstein had added a comprehensive appendix to his dramas as well. His novel *Arminius* is probably the best example of a courtly-historical novel functioning as a seventeenth-century encyclopedia. Historical, philosophical, and religious essays and discussions are interspersed throughout the novel, not to mention the fact that Germanic, Roman, and Middle Eastern customs of various kinds are described with considerable historical accuracy. It is the author's intent to familiarize the reader with sundry knowledge about the world, familiarizing him at the same time with the countries and cultures of the various peoples which take part in the action. That Lohenstein had poetic abilities cannot be denied, but a good part of his *Arminius* is the work of a scholar and man of letters. The novel is a compilation of the views and the knowledge of the seventeenth century, be it in political, philosophical, religious, or historical matters.

Patriotic historiography, which made Germanic antiquity the focus for national pride, is a fruit of sixteenth-century Humanism. It was stimulated by *Germania,* a report by the Roman historian Cornelius Tacitus (A.D. 55-116). Tacitus also reports the events surrounding the battle in the Teutoburg Forest (A.D. 9) (*Annales*), which form the basis for an Arminius cult, found in German literature beginning with Ulrich von Hutten (1488-1523). To many German poets, Arminius is the symbol of national independence, liberty, and unity, a symbol of the struggle against the tremendous political and cultural influence of the Romance countries and cultures in Germany. This influence was a present and often-lamented fact throughout the seventeenth century. As is demonstrated by the later dramas of Klopstock, Kleist, and Grabbe, all dealing with the battle in the Teutoburg Forest, the patriotic feelings of the Germans were aroused by this topic, and its hero was exalted by legend.

Lohenstein's main intention is the glorification of Germanic antiquity and, thus, of the Germans in contrast to the Romans.[23] For him, the Germans form the pedestal on which world history stands. The Roman Empire therefore derived its power from the Germanic tribes serving under its banners. All those peoples against whom the Romans fought unsuccessfully turn out to be Germanic ones. Thus, Lohenstein's novel turns Roman historiography upside down and becomes a conscious countermanifesto against the self-glorification of Rome.[24] The novelist draws the picture of a Golden Age of the Germans with an advanced and flourishing culture, which is extremely remote from the primitivism of the Germans found in Tacitus' writings. In Lohenstein's work, the Germanic priests have knowledge and philosophical insights which outshine Greek or Roman wisdom. Germany appears to be much better than its reputation would have it. It is by no means the barbaric, desolate wilderness, as the envious Roman historians want to make the reader believe; rather, the Germanic nations possess a cultural and political power equal to the other empires of antiquity. The courtly culture described here has more similarity with seventeenth-century culture than with the Germanic culture at the time of Arminius. German Baroque culture has been projected into the culture of Germanic antiquity and idealized in the process. The empirical science and philosophy of the seventeenth century appear before the reader in Germanic garb. However, in Lohenstein's description what is missing are the vices, the intrigues, and the moral decay.

With this healthy Germanic world, Lohenstein has contrasted the Roman and Middle Eastern world as unhealthy and decadent —in short, as a negative counterpart. Whereas the Germany of antiquity is, for Lohenstein, consciously or unconsciously, the symbol of everything bright, positive, and good, Rome is the symbol of all dark and evil powers.[25] Ceremonial pomp, seventeenth-century sensualism, and the Machiavellistic counsels of Balthasar Gracián are incorporated into the Mediterranean cultures. However, whereas Lohenstein rather lightly depicts the Germans' virtuousness, liberty, and simplicity in a colorless fashion, he depicts the depravity and viciousness of Rome in the brightest tones. The Rome of the time of Emperor Augustus, who, by the way, is depicted as a vicious sensualist, appears to be completely orientalized—a historical inaccuracy, as Rome at the time of Augustus had not yet been influenced by Oriental customs to that extent. It is understood that the legendary rather than historically ascertainable depravity of Emperor Tiberius is taken for granted. Thus, Rome is used as a metaphor for vice. The word symbolism of the anagram Roma-Amor comes to the aid of the poet. Lohenstein, to be sure, condemns the display of fantastic splendor, garments, gems, cruelties, lusts and passions, parties and erotic orgies, but he appears to do this almost too eagerly, obviously being unable to avoid their exotic attraction. His imagination revels in the description of the court of the Thracian queen Ada, who is performing the "science of vices," having "scrutinized all its secrets." With sophistic dialectics he has the epicurean princely guardian in Rome state, as the most profound truth, that there is no god—a dangerous secret which has to be kept concealed from the rabble. The stoicism of the hero Arminius is contrasted with the epicurean hedonism of the Roman libertines. Rome is the negative foil which serves to reveal healthy Germany even more clearly.

However, *Arminius* is not only a piece of biased historiography in novel form, but also in part a *roman à clef*.[26] Arminius himself is supposed to represent the German Emperor Leopold; Drusus the French King Louis XIV, indeed the entire dynasty of Hapsburg emperors, ending with Leopold, is represented under Germanic names in Arminius' pedigree. In the case of *Arminius, roman à clef* means that the most recent history of Europe has been projected into that of Germanic antiquity. Thus, in disguise are encountered also Luther and the denominational adversaries of the sixteenth and the seventeenth centuries, the Massacre of St. Bartholomew, the most recent history of Sweden and of England with its revolution are also encountered in disguise. It is a sign of Lohenstein's virtuosity as a writer that he is able to switch the identifications of his characters with historical figures. When Lohenstein no longer considers the identification of one of his figures with a figure of modern history suitable, he changes the reference to another historical person or allows the story to continue as a mere fiction—a change that is often revealed in the notes. Thus, Divitiacus stands at one point for Luther; at another point, for King Henry VIII of England. It is on account of his virtuosity that the intellectual freedom, the esthetically playful element of the writer Lohenstein rises above that of his contemporaries.[27] He thus widens the delinea-

tion of Germanic history into a history of Europe and into a
lofty historical construction of a special type.

Critics ordinarily see in Duke Anton Ulrich's and Lohenstein's
novels the highest achievements of the courtly-historical novel
in Germany. This is generally true; in Lohenstein's case the
judgment must be modified, however. As far as style and structure are concerned, *Arminius* is without a doubt a courtly-
historical novel, but encyclopedic and patriotic tendencies play
such a major role in it that the actual plot, ruled by the anonymous *Verhängnis* (fate), is entirely relegated to the background.[28]
Thus, the novel has become a receptacle for various literary
forms of different genres, which are difficult to fit into the
courtly-historical superstructure, and the philosophical discourse, the dialogue, and the discussion of historical facts or of
general problems very easily attain a certain independence.

Even elements of the pastoral novel have permeated *Arminius*, as the following plot summary demonstrates: Marbod, ruler
of the Boians, is injured in a fight in the Sudetic Mountains and
is taken to a hermit's cavern by two faithful followers. The
form of a *Fürstenspiegel* crystallizes when the hermit turns out
to be Ariovist (a German chieftain thought to be dead), who
then instructs Marbod in politics. Ariovist leads his guests into
a grotto in the *Riesengebirge,* where a mummy of the German
progenitor Tuisco is kept. The grotto also represents the center
of the system of Silesian rivers. Marbod and his companions
meet spirits of the water, of the forest, and of the air, and after
Ariovist's death they meet a herbalist. They finally arrive at
a shepherds' festival where the Schaffgotsch family is paid hom-
age. This summary not only demonstrates the fact that many elements of the pastoral novel have permeated Lohenstein's work
but also shows its literary dependence on Opitz' *Schäfferey von
der Nimfen Hercinie.*

In contrast to other courtly-historical novels, the action of
Arminius occupies about ten years. Although a segment of history that actually extended over a much longer period of time
has been concentrated and projected into this time span, the
strict formal limitations of the courtly-historical novel are
exceeded here. Furthermore, it would have been easy for Lohenstein to put the Varus battle in the Teutoburg Forest at the end
of the novel rather than at its beginning. Then he would have

been able to culminate Arminius' life with his greatest success. Placing it at the beginning, he not only has to camouflage or quickly pass over numerous defeats, but contrary to history— he was murdered by his own relatives—Arminius has to live on as the prince of the Marcomans. Correspondingly, history has to be altered with regard to Thusnelda, who by no means returned safely home to Germany, but died as a Roman prisoner. Also because of the chosen time span, Lohenstein passes up the opportunity to have his novel end in a final apotheosis complete with wedding and victory. Thus, it becomes obvious that the urge to write about German history and to glorify it once more relegates some of the generic requirements to the background.

VI   *Heinrich Anshelm von Zigler und Kliphausen,*
Die Asiatische Banise

One of the prime examples of a courtly-historical novel is a work which may be called the most popular one of its time, the influence of which extended well into the nineteenth century:[29] Heinrich Anshelm von Zigler und Kliphausen's novel *Die Asiatische Banise / Oder Das blutig= doch muthige Pegu.* First published in 1689, the novel was republished in numerous editions. Johann Georg Hamann, an uncle of the famous precursor of the Storm and Stress, honored it by writing a sequel;[30] several imitations appeared, among them an *Englische Banise,*[31] as well as at least three dramatizations.

In this case, the author's identity is not concealed behind a pseudonym but in the obvious initials of his full name: Heinrich Anshelm von Zigler und Kliphausen (1663-96) was a Lusatian nobleman. Beginning in 1682 he was a student in Frankfurt a.O.; in 1684, however, after the death of his father, he returned home. He married, and during the remaining years of his relatively short life he bought and resold one manor after the other. Zigler himself led by no means as colorful a life as he describes in his novel, but in spite of the vicinity of the Baroque court of the Saxon elector August the Strong, he was a bookworm. In addition to *Asiatische Banise,* he published a volume of poems in 1691, entitled *Helden-Liebe der Schrift;* in 1695 his *Täglicher Schauplatz der Zeit* appeared; and in 1701, posthumously, the *Historisches Labyrinth der Zeit,* which was completed by an editor, was published. The last two publications are profuse encyclopedic compilations. These works are related to the voluminous collections of curiosities which were so popular at the end of that century.

In Zigler we encounter once again a type of Baroque author frequently found among the novelists and poets of that time, that is, an author who enjoys financial independence because of his station, his position, or his inherited fortune, and who makes the writing of books a diverting and pleasant pastime. The plot of *Asiatische Banise,* which shall be the only one of the courtly-historical novels we wish to discuss in detail, is as follows:

Prince Balacin of Ava, who is searching for his fiancée Banise, the princess of Pegu, is attacked by the followers of the tyrant Chaumigrem, and is wounded. He recovers in the castle of Talemon, who is a faithful partisan of the former Emperor of Pegu, Xemindo, Banise's father. Scandor, Balacin's servant and friend, arrives unexpectedly, bringing the news that Balacin has inherited two kingdoms.

Following this, Scandor relates the life history of Prince Balacin and his sister, Princess Higvanama: Balacin's father had become friends with the scheming general, Chaumigrem, who was attempting to win the Princess Higvanama (engaged to Prince Nherandi of Siam). When Balacin tries to protect his sister from the insolent Chaumigrem, he is exiled by his father.

Thereupon Scandor tells the *Lieb- und Lebensgeschichte Prinz Balacins und der Prinzessin Banise*: A mysterious oracle prophesies to the prince that he will find his happiness in Pegu. On his way there he saves the life of the emperor of that country, who has been ambushed by a band of robbers hired by Chaumigrem. At the court of Pegu, Balacin falls in love with Princess Banise, whose life he saves from a panther that had escaped from its cage. He reveals his identity, and he and Banise become engaged. Back in Ava, he is imprisoned by his father, while Chaumigrem, in the meantime, conquers Pegu.

At this point, Talemon relates *Tod und Untergang des unglückseligen Kaisers Xemindo samt dessen Prinzen und ganzen Reich*: During the conquest of Pegu, numerous people, including the emperor himself, are publicly executed. Abaxar, a high-ranking officer, receives the order to kill Banise; he supposedly carries out this order in the inner court of his home, and then he has the headless body taken to the marketplace. As Talemon relates this, Abaxar, who is present, is arrested by Chaumigrem's troops. He confesses to having saved the princess by executing a slave in her place. Banise is arrested in Abaxar's home and is brought before Chaumigrem. He expresses his desire to marry her and gives her six days to agree.

Balacin, who in the meantime has fully recovered from his wounds, disguises himself as a Portuguese merchant and manages to be admitted to Banise's quarters along with Scandor. His attempt to abduct her fails; Balacin escapes, but Banise and Scandor are caught by Chaumigrem's men.

While Balacin is raising an army against Chaumigrem in his native country, Chaumigrem conquers Siam by means of unprecedented cruelty. Prince Nherandi and his sister are captured. Meanwhile, Banise is left in the custody of the old Rolim, the high priest, who loves her himself. She stabs him to death when he attempts to accost her physically.

In the war against Chaumigrem, Balacin wins the decisive battle and lays the city of Pegu under siege. Banise is supposed to be sacrificed on the altar of the war god. With Abaxar's aid, Balacin secretly enters the city, becomes a priest, and when Banise is supposed to be sacrificed, he stabs Chaumigrem at the altar. The city of Pegu is taken by Balacin's troups. Balacin is crowned Emperor of Pegu and marries Banise. King Nherandi of Siam marries Balacin's sister Higvanama; Abaxar, who turns out to be Prince Palkim of Prom, who had fled from Chaumigrem, marries Nherandi's sister. On the occasion of the wedding celebrations, the Portuguese perform a play which concludes the novel. The play is entitled *Die Handlung der listigen Rache oder der tapfere Heraclius.*

This plot is, in many respects, confusing, though in comparison with the extensive novels of Duke Anton Ulrich, Lohenstein, and Buchholtz, it is easy to follow. Zigler did not invent the plot himself, but based it on historical sources, which he quotes in the introduction and in several footnotes. His main sources are the voluminous writings of the productive Erasmus Francisci from Nuremberg: *Ost- und West-Indischer wie auch Sinesischer Lust- und Staats-Garten* (1668) and *Neu-polierter Geschichts- Kunst- und Sitten-Spiegel ausländischer Völker* (1670).

The scholar from Nuremberg, of course, had not witnessed the sixteenth-century events in Indochina himself, but he had extensively utilized eyewitness reports of the Portuguese conquistador Fernand Mendez Pinto (1509-83), who from 1537 to 1558, had traveled extensively in Indochina and China as a soldier, pirate, servant, and beggar.[32] In his monograph on *Die Asiatische Banise*[33] as well as in his *Nachwort* (interpretive essay) to his modern reprint of the novel (=*AB*), Wolfgang Pfeiffer-Belli has compared history and novel meticulously, ascertaining that Zigler has incorporated a large number of historical facts in his novel, even in the more minute details. However, with regard to genre affiliation, not the facts but rather deviations from historical accuracy are of particular interest. Under the name of Chaumigrem, for example, the despotic activities of several tyrants are combined in one figure. The tyrant Chaumigrem was actually preceded by another tyrant by the name of Xemimbrum, who in the novel is only mentioned in Scandor's narration as supposedly being Chaumigrem's brother. The historical Chaumigrem was not punished by the just revenge of heaven; rather, he died a natural death in 1583, in full possession of his power. It was his son whose armies, in 1599, were surrounded by the neighboring kings of Ava, Arakan, Tangu, and Siam and who was killed by them. As is evident from these facts, Zigler has compressed the historical events of a fifty-year period into a short time span. The historically benevolent King Xemindo did indeed have a daughter who was engaged to the prince of Ava; this relationship, however, did not have a happy ending. By order of Chaumigrem, she was strangled on the back of her father who had fainted and collapsed.

Although Zigler, for the most part, preserves the historical background, it is obvious that as far as the actual plot of the novel is concerned, he follows the generic requirements of the courtly-historical novel. In accordance with these rules, a fictional love story becomes the center of action. Amidst all the complicated ups and downs of the political events in sixteenth-century Indochina, *der gerechten Himmel* ("just heaven"), *die Vorsehung* ("Providence"), *die Götter* ("the gods"), or whatever the good principle may be called, proves to be victorious, bringing the two lovers together "to live happily ever after." Although the couple Balacin-Banise forms the sole center of attention, the novel ends with several weddings between the princes and princesses, in accordance with the structural principle of the courtly-historical novel. As far as the method of presentation is concerned, the principle of relating antecedent events following an action-packed beginning is typical of the genre. This is realized in several stories: "Lebensgeschichte Prinz Balacins und der Prinzessin Higvanama," "Lieb- und Lebensgeschichte Prinz Balacins und der Prinzessin Banisen," and "Geschichte von Tod und Untergang des unglückseligen Kaisers Xemindo." In conjunction with this technique, the *in medias res* technique employed here is probably the best example of its kind.[34] The novel starts, so to speak, with a beat of the kettledrum, an emotional outburst of the lonely prince Balacin, which is typical for the style of the entire novel:

Blitz, Donner und Hagel, als die rächenden Werkzeuge des gerechten Himmels, zerschmettere den Pracht deiner goldbedeckten Türme, und die Rache der Götter verzehre alle Besitzer der Stadt: welche den Untergang des Königlichen Hauses befördert, oder nicht solchen nach äußerstem Vermögen, auch mit Darsetzung ihres Blutes, gebührend verhindert haben. Wollten die Götter! es könnten meine Augen zu donnerschwangern Wolken, und diese meine Tränen zu grausamen Sündfluten werden: [...] (*AB*, p. 15)

Lightning, thunder, and hail, as the revenging tools of just heaven, crush the splendor of your gold-covered towers, and the revenge of the gods may destroy all owners of this city: who have furthered the extinction of the Royal House, or who have not sufficiently endeavored to prevent such action with all their power, even by risking their lives. If only the gods would let my eyes become clouds heavy with thunder, and these my tears torrential deluges: [...]

Zigler, to be sure, states in his preface ("Nach Standes-Gebühr Geehrter Leser"), that he consistently strove to employ a light and simple style (*AB*, p. 13),[35] but sentences such as the ones quoted above, filled with superlativistic metaphors, apparently discredit this attempt. The author definitely writes in the high, sometimes stilted, and sometimes bombastic style of the courtly-historical novel. His style often borders on the grotesque, as for example, in the description of the archvillain Chaumigrem, who is described as a misshapen, ugly dwarf with bad breath (*AB*, p. 56). In his battle descriptions, Zigler appears to indulge in fantastic exaggerations. Piles of bodies bar the passage of the troops besieging the cities, and hundreds of thousands are slaughtered in a single battle. The cruelty of the victor who marches into a conquered city appears limitless. Thousands of people are executed by his order in the cruelest manner. At one time, Chaumigrem goes so far as to give the order to collect the corpses of babies and small children, lying in the streets, and throw them to the elephants along with rice and grass (*AB*, p. 212). Descriptions of such cruelties are typical of the style of the novel, but almost all of them can also be found in the author's sources. Apart from exaggerated descriptions of Oriental customs, exemplified by incredibly high numbers—to the German reader of the seventeenth century reports of armies numbering six hundred thousand to seven hundred thousand must have sounded incredible—we also find descriptions of Oriental customs, such as in funerals, sacrifices to the gods, legal actions, and so forth, which (another ingredient of the courtly-historical novel) occur in a similar form in Zesen's *Assenat*. This feature not only adds local color but also satisfies our sense of historical authenticity as well as the seventeenth-century reader's encyclopedic interest. Naturally these insertions are compiled from the author's readings, once again demonstrating how many historical and geographical sources Zigler must have read in order to write this single work.

One could easily get the impression that the action of the novel is remote from seventeenth-century life and that the author, by consciously indulging in exotisms, was forgetting his own time. This is entirely wrong—*Die Asiatische Banise,* to be sure, is no *roman à clef*, depicting, in exotic garb, specific seventeenth-century events and circumstances. However, the purposely Orientalized, exotic Indochinese characteristics are matched by those features which, in Oriental disguise, mirror the author's present time. The fact that the hero and the heroine represent seventeenth-century European ideals is shown in the constancy of their love, their virtue, and their heroism. They are characteristic types of the period and, as such, are typical characters of the courtly-historical novel. In addition, the courts of Indochina are socially structured like European courts, with a similar order of rank, ceremony, and behavior of the characters. Lovers dispatch to each other letters including enamored poetic discourses and assure one another of their mutual faithfulness.

It is not only the personal conduct of the characters that displays traits of Zigler's own time but also the political philosophy, the concept of monarchy, and the system of states. As the subtitle asserts, at the end Balacin may rise, like the *Reichs-Sonne*, the "sun of the empire," which had set with the good emperor Xemindo. The absolutist political order of Indochina is compared to the system of the planets circling around the sun (*AB*, p. 417),[36] exactly as Zigler's contemporaries viewed the French King Louis XIV and the other European states. The speech which Rolim delivers at the end of the novel on the occasion of Balacin's coronation enumerates all the positive attributes of a prince: reason, justice, virtue, good reputation, bravery, piety, wisdom, constancy, prudence, a peace-loving nature and so on. This speech is a *Fürstenspiegel* (discourse on the qualities of a prince) in a nutshell.

The villain Chaumigrem, who is depicted as the castigating scourge of the angered gods (*AB*, pp. 157, 321) intrudes into the planetary system of the courts and their good princes. He appears as would a comet, a *Schwanzstern*, an apparent aberration in the divine order. Characterizing in contrasting black and white, Zigler attributes to him the vices of immoderate ambition, jealousy and cruelty. In turn, he contrasts the virtues of a ruler mentioned above with the *ratio status,* the reason of state. Programmatically, Chaumigrem replies to the high priest, Rolim, who advises him to show kindness and justice, that there cannot be any law which would limit the power of a free king, and that *ratio status* is the only guiding principle for a ruler (*AB*, pp. 233, 261). Thus, the events of the novel, taken together, are viewed as an exemplary case, a wicked ruler being contrasted with a good one.

Not only the political philosophy of the novel is courtly-Baroque, but so is its end. Portuguese singers and actors perform an Italian opera, *Die listige Rache oder der tapfere Heraclius*. This play of Zigler's, which allegedly was performed in Pegu, is actually a plagiarism. It is the translation of an original Italian libretto, which was translated into German by the Silesian dramatist Johann Christian Hallmann (1640-1704).[37] By including this opera, Zigler does not perform a *"saltomortale* into the world of the opera" but rather expresses relief and happiness over the joyous resolution of the intricacies of the plot. Zigler's opera is a *Festspiel* or *Freudenspiel* of the kind Gryphius wrote for similar occasions. Correspondingly, Zigler has not selected an opera at random; he has chosen one with a plot that transposes the theme of the novel into the mythological realm and which repeats the parallel events on a legendary-mythological plane. Just as, in the novel, Banise is kept a prisoner by Chaumigrem and freed by Balacin, in the opera, Phocas, the tyrant of Constantinople, is holding prisoner the princess Theodosia, daughter of the imprisoned emperor. She is freed by Heraclius, the son of Heracleonas, who kills the tyrant Phocas in the same way in which Balacin kills Chaumigrem. The plot of the novel and that of the opera are so strikingly similar in their basic structure that it seems justified to question whether Zigler might have transposed the structure from the opera, which he had at hand, to the events of Indochina, which he knew from his sources. There is another reason, however, why an *excursion* into the world of opera cannot be considered here; opera and *Festspiel* are an integral part and an expression of courtly society, not only as a literary form, but also as cultural elements per se. As the courtly-historical novel glorifies courtly class ideals, demonstrating their validity against a martial-heroic background, the opera focuses its attention on the splendor of the love story, often combined with pastoral elements. The close relation of both genres to each other becomes especially evident by their juxtaposition in *Die Asiatische Banise*.

Within the novel itself we find traits of another type of novel, which have been introduced into the courtly-historical novel, and which, in this case, are even more striking than, for example, in Grimmelshausen's *Keuscher Joseph*: elements of the picaresque novel. Prince Balacin's servant and friend Scandor, to be sure, is of noble birth, but in his entire behavior he is still a *picaro*, so that, for example, in the adaptations for the eighteenth-century stage he could easily be fitted into the role of a *Hanswurst*, a buffoon. It is typical, for example, that he represents his master in a nightly visit paid to Balacin by the lovesick Lorangy, Talemon's stepdaughter, allowing himself to be married to her in bed, a scene, which, without doubt, was influenced by Grimmelshausen's *Simplicissimus*. Scandor's adventures with the malodorous wife of the supervisor of the elephants can also be considered picaresque, as can the scene in which he, disguised as a Portuguese merchant, teases the women at the court of Pegu—an incident which is reminiscent of the quack scenes in the Spanish and German picaresque novels. Numerous elements of style, as they appear in the parts which Scandor narrates, correspond to those found in the style of the picaresque novels, so that, by introducing Scandor, the picaresque elements in style and plot form a counterbalance to the serious courtly-historical tone of the Balacin-Banise action. The tragedy of the destruction of the empires and the love of the hero and the heroine is contrasted with the playful comedy of the page Scandor, whereas the *Festspiel* about the brave Heraclius adds a happy end to everything. That does not mean, however, that *Die Asiatische Banise* is not a courtly-historical novel, but it shows that, in spite of the rigid generic requirements of the seventeenth century, other elements had intruded into the courtly-historical genre.

VII   *Hans Jacob Christoffel von Grimmelshausen:*
Keuscher Joseph

Biblical themes had always enjoyed great popularity in German literature, not only throughout the Middle Ages but also in the sixteenth century, during which time the Humanist dramatists repeatedly chose topics from the Scriptures. For this reason there are numerous dramatizations of the Susanna theme, of the Parable of the Prodigal Son, and of the Joseph story.

In addition, the authors of the seventeenth-century courtly-historical novels were also interested in such themes, on the one hand because the source of the theme guaranteed beforehand absolute authenticity; and on the other because the conciseness of the biblical report allowed the author the opportunity to draw on his own fantasy. Not too many biblical themes lent themselves that readily to a transformation into a courtly-historical novel, either because the Bible did not provide enough factual information, or because the story did not have a theme or a structure which was required by the genre.

The favorite biblical theme of the German Baroque novelists was the Joseph story. The topic lent itself to treatment within a novel for several reasons: as a setting, Palestine and

Egypt were as enticing as Indochina or Syria; too, the topic offered numerous opportunities for elaborating on the customs, habits, and ceremonies of the ancient Egyptians. More important, however, was the fact that the biblical account already contained several elements which fulfilled the generic requirements of the courtly-historical novel. Regarding the scene in which Potiphar's wife attempts to seduce Joseph, the action not only contained the element of erotic love but, at the same time, incorporated the motif of the hero's temptation. In addition, Joseph's rise to the second most powerful man of the state fulfilled the requirement that the novel should also concern itself with affairs of state. By virtue of these elements, the action had a happy ending; however, this action had to be supplemented in several respects in order to be able to fit into the traditional structural scheme.[38] Joseph needed to have a female counterpart, a partner—Assenat—a personality barely mentioned in the Bible. Assenat, to be sure, could be introduced at an early stage as a character; however, she had to remain in the background until after the attempted seduction by Potiphar's wife in order to reserve for this scene the nature of the great test of virtue. Even more was necessary to complete the adaptation. In the Bible, Joseph was the son of a patriarch of herdsmen. Consequently, he had to be raised socially, becoming the son of an old and powerful family, equal in rank to princes. Correspondingly, Assenat is made a princess, the daughter of the Egyptian high priest, and Potiphar appears as a high dignitary.

The theme was treated in various ways, depending on the character of the author. The treatment by Grimmelshausen and Zesen will demonstrate the possibilities of variation within a given theme and a given genre.

Des Vortrefflich Keuschen Josephs in Egypten Lebensbeschreibung (1667) was Grimmelshausen's first novel. As such, it displays several technical and stylistic weaknesses, but *in nuce* it already contains elements which will subsequently characterize Grimmelshausen: his popular style and his humor, his moralizing, the discussion of man's relation to God, the contrasting of a positive and a negative man, and the character of the adventurer, an influence from the picaresque novel.

In prefatory remarks addressed to the reader, the author

points out that he is basing his novel on various sources in addition to the Bible (Gen. 1: 37 and 39-50), having compiled from these sources whatever material did not contradict the Bible (*KJ*, p. 5). He expressly mentions the Jewish historian Flavius Josephus (*Jüdische Altertümer*, Bk. II, Chaps. 2-4); the Near Eastern and Persian versions of the Joseph legend can be identified as further sources, especially the *Haggadic Interpretation of the Genesis* and Sepher Hajaschar, on whose writing the twelfth sura of the Koran is based. Grimmelshausen himself refers the reader to Adam Olearius' *Orientalische Reisebeschreibung* (first edition, 1647), to which he is supposedly indebted for the name of Potiphar's wife, Selicha. However, this statement is incorrect, as the work does not mention anyone by the name of Selicha. Grimmelshausen can only be referring to Sheik Saadi's *Persianisches Rosenthal* which had been translated by Olearius and which, in many editions, had been added to the *Orientalische Reisebeschreibung*.[39]

It is obvious that Grimmelshausen added relatively little to the events reported in the Book of Genesis. For him the Joseph story is *not* a courtly-historical novel. Even in its narrative technique his *Keuscher Joseph* differs from the courtly-historical novel. Grimmelshausen narrates in correct chronological order, without employing the *in medias res* technique, that is, telling later what has happened previously. Just as the affair with Assenat, whom Grimmelshausen calls Asaneth, plays a subordinate part only, the principle of doubling the couples has also been excluded. In addition, the elements typical of the courtly-historical novel have only marginal importance: the recounting of Joseph's rise to power is relatively short, except when he displays his wealth as the host of his brothers. A description of Egyptian customs, architecture, and so on is almost entirely lacking. Only the appendix, which contains the biography of Joseph's friend Musai, contains several of these elements. Grimmelshausen's *Keuscher Joseph* is, just like Genesis, on the one hand a family history, an embellished and enlarged paraphrase of biblical events. On the other hand it is, like the biblical story, an *exemplum*, that is, an exemplary description of the behavior of a man who is tempted, and the subsequent demonstration of Divine Providence. Here, in his first work, Grimmelshausen introduces himself immediately as a moralist. This didactic-

moralistic message is clearly expressed in the publisher's adver-
tisements in the catalogues of the book fairs of Frankfurt and
Leipzig of 1665 and 1666; it states, for example:

Exempel der unveränderlichen Vorsehung Gottes / unter einer
anmuthigen und ausführlichen Histori dem keuschen Joseph in
Egypten [. . .] (*KJ*, p. VIII)[40]

Example of the constant providence of God, embodied in a graceful
and detailed story; the Chaste Joseph in Egypt [. . .]

In the plot summary, which precedes the novel, the author
states, interpreting the novel as a whole:

Damit aber Jacob und seine Kinder zu ihrer Ankunft [in Egypt]
auch Unterschleiff und Lebens=Mittel finden möchten / hat die
Göttliche ohnveränderliche Vorsehung Jacobs liebsten / weisesten
und schönsten Sohn Joseph / den seine Brüder verkaufften / vor
ihm her gesandt / [. . .] (*KJ*, p. 6)

In order to provide food and shelter for Jacob and his children upon
their arrival [in Egypt], the divine and unchanging providence has
sent ahead Jacob's dearest, wisest and most beautiful son Joseph,
whom his brothers had sold. [. . .]

It is stressed several times that the brothers merely follow
God's providence in selling Joseph (*KJ*, pp. 7, 113, 123) and
thus cannot actually be considered guilty. Man is God's
tool; his actions, whether good or evil, are directed by God's
higher intent. This is the implied message of Grimmelshausen's
novel. In accordance with this message, Grimmelshausen expresses the didactic lesson in the last paragraph of the novel
by admonishing the readers of the novel as well to entrust
themselves to God's constant providence (*KJ*, p 125). The
biblical message of the novel is thus transformed into a moral
demand.

Joseph also knows that his brothers, as well as he himself,
are tools of God's plan, of His direction. The goal of his life
has been set already in his early adolescence: he is the chosen
one of God's chosen people. This fact is demonstrated by his
extraordinary beauty, by his prudence, and by his virtue. Joseph
himself realizes his future glory through his own dreams, which
his father interprets for him. These dreams are an element

which the poet has purposely reinforced. To the dreams, Grimmelshausen has added the prophecies, based on the astrological
and chiromantic knowledge of Musai (who was the leader of the
Ismailian caravan and later on Joseph's personal manager), and
on Potiphar's oracle which prophesies trouble for him in case
he were to marry a second time. Prophecies and their fulfillment
had been popular since the late Greek novel. In Grimmelshausen's *Keuscher Joseph* they enclose the entire novel like a
net, being in themselves independent literary forms. However,
they are not simply an element of form which supports the
structure of the plot by adding a narrative structure; they
also reinforce the message of the novel. They are the manifestation of providence, a gradual confirmation of the divine plan
underlying the development of the action. Divine Providence
signifies its omnipresence by the characters' various methods
of predicting the future. *Because* Joseph firmly believes in his
dreams, he gains the inner strength to bear his changing fate,
to endure it by maintaining his virtue. From his knowledge of
his portentous future, Joseph, the wise one, derives his inner
security, his tranquillity of mind, so that he is able to reconcile
himself with the unavoidable without despairing. Equipped
with the Baroque virtues of magnanimity and constancy, he
stands above the changeability of the world. Through this feeling of assurance in the conviction of faith, the knowledge of
God's omnipresence, the dominance of the goddess Fortuna of
the courtly-historical novel is eliminated. In this respect, Joseph
presents himself as the worldly-wise man who, inside himself,
has overcome the inconstancy of the world. He does not once
(as do the heroes of *Die Asiatische Banise*) curse his fate,
because fate does not exist for him. He endures the change
from the favorite son of the rich and powerful Jacob to a slave,
then to a supervisor and favorite of Potiphar, to a smith's helper
in prison, and finally to the second most powerful man in the
state, secure in the knowledge that he will be cared for by
God's providence. Thus, he stands as the ideal Baroque hero.

Just as Dietwald is tempted by the devil in disguise of the
hermit and Proximus in the person of his greedy uncle, Joseph,
too, is led into temptation—not simply by words, but by the
immediate, sensual presence of Selicha, his master Potiphar's
young wife. Step by step, Grimmelshausen leads Joseph, and

consequently the reader as well, to this scene of seduction, which is described in detail, in which Joseph, by virtue of his unshakable belief in God, succeeds in tearing himself away from the lovesick Selicha, leaving behind only his coat. Again a comparison with *Simplicissimus* lends itself to consideration. Simplicius did not succeed in overcoming his own lusts by fleeing from his love intrigues in Paris. Grimmelshausen signifies this violation of a Christian commandment by the loss of external beauty as a result of smallpox. Joseph is offered sensual pleasure in the form of beautiful colors, female nudity, sweet scents, and coaxing words—he flees, and his own external beauty increases in spite of his hard physical work as a blacksmith's helper in prison. This shows that Simplicius and Joseph are two opposite types, distinguished by their different behavior, and by their different reactions to temptation. Whereas Grimmelshausen's picaresque novel allows its hero to sin, not allowing him to experience self-understanding and purification of his mind before the conclusion, in the static courtly-historical novel the hero, from the very beginning, is equipped to fight temptation by means of virtue.[41] Whereas the picaresque hero Simplicius goes through various stages of development, Joseph does not change; he simply proves himself. The basic theme here is temptation of sensual pleasures and self-control through virtue, which is directly founded in the belief in God: in prayer Joseph finds the strength to resist temptation (*KJ*, p. 56). In overcoming the affects and passions, he again proves to be the ideal Baroque hero.

Before Joseph is redeemed, however, he is humbled by being sent innocently to prison.[42] In this way as well he becomes an exemplary Christian hero. Even though later, in the story of Musai, he emphatically rejects the identification with Christ (*KJ*, p. 162), Grimmelshausen renders his hero in many respects a Christ figure: In contrast to Grimmelshausen's sources, Joseph's brothers sell him for thirty pieces of silver rather than for twenty. Joseph not only appears to the caravan as a saving god (Apollo) but also as the savior of Egypt and of his own people. Beyond these external aspects, he demonstrates superhuman qualities: he not only has the ability to accept his fate voluntarily and not to curse it, he also practices the Golden Rule of the New Testament—"Love thy enemy"—not only in the disguise of the god Apollo protecting his brothers from the Arab robbers but also by refusing to accuse Selicha, although he has the incriminating letter which she sent to him in prison. This behavior becomes most obvious when his brothers arrive in Egypt. Whereas Musai, as a worldly man, immediately sees an opportunity for punishment, Joseph is ready for forgiveness and reconciliation. He now makes the same demand on his brothers as God made on him: to overcome themselves by self-sacrifice and by fighting for their brother Benjamin. Thus, Joseph's brothers also demonstrate what the poet had previously shown through Joseph himself—that he who overcomes himself can be redeemed.

Joseph's antagonist is Potiphar's wife Selicha. We may justifiably interpret her as the embodiment of seductive beauty and, at the same time, of the sinfulness of this world. But she is no allegorical *Frau Welt* like Courasche, for example, but in her passionate obsession, which becomes increasingly animalistic, she reveals very human traits. In contrast to Joseph she stands for the man who cannot resist the attraction of lust or temptation. Thus, she can only react by crying when Asaneth confronts her with reproaches, not being able to resist her passions (*KJ*, pp. 47 f.). Whereas Joseph remains the same in his constant virtue, Selicha undergoes a change. The young woman who adores the handsome slave is transformed into a devilish fury, who, under the impetus of passions, becomes an animal and no longer shuns criminal acts (*KJ*, pp. 62 f.). However, again it would be wrong to interpret this change as an inner development of her soul. What takes place is a process of self-destruction; she is lacerated by the passions which are named by the author: anger, love, passion, remorse, and the fear that her crime might be discovered (*KJ*, p. 70), the whole Baroque arsenal of destructive emotions.

In *Der Keusche Joseph*, there is one character who does not fit into the genre of the courtly-historical novel: Musai, the leader of the Ismailian caravan and later Joseph's personal manager. In an appendix to the novel which was written and published later, Musai is introduced more fully, but in the novel itself he already has his characteristic qualities. He is a character who has entered from the poet's picaresque world into his courtly one, a *picaro*. Thanks to Musai's inventive genius, the caravan is saved from the Arabic robbers. He operates with the cunning, the tricks, and the experience of a man who "has been through the mill," who has experienced the inconstancy of human affairs, indeed, who knows that in human life there is nothing constant but inconstancy itself. He has gathered wealth and lost it again; he was a wealthy merchant, a leader of caravans, a slave, and ends up as a prince after he has found the true god. He differs from the *picaro* of the Spanish picaresque novel, who has no goal, in that he has to a great degree developed a view for essentials during his long life, which was so rich in changes. Not only the sympathy Grimmelshausen ascribed to him, but, above all, his position as Joseph's personal manager, suggests that the poet has endowed him with personal traits.[43]

The presence of legendary courtly-historical and picaresque elements in the characters of the novel corresponds to the confounding of the two styles, without their being bound to corresponding characters. The gallant, courtly elements of style do not abound; stylized language and language formulas are to be found extremely rarely; such instances as the color of Joseph's face, for example, remind Grimmelshausen of a mixture of rose and lily leaves; Selicha's breasts appear as white as alabaster (*KJ,* p. 56) or snow white; Joseph's admonishing words are "wie lauter Blitz und Donnerschlag" (*KJ,* p. 59) ("like pure thunder and lightning"). The vigorous, popular tone of the picaresque novel, which is so characteristic for Grimmelshausen, already exists in this the author's first work. There is no indulgence in anything stilted or exotic, but rather the attempt to assimilate everything foreign to the familiar German atmosphere. Selicha talks in "austrücklichen teutschen Worten" (*KJ,* p. 44) ("in clear German words"), and Musai has "nach der Elamiter Art einen offenhertzigen Teutschen Sinn" (*KJ,* p. 84) ("according to the character of the Elamites an open German mind").[44] Or note the beautiful anachronism:

Asaneth verfügte sich heim / und schetzte / daß sie desselben Tag mehr gefischt hätte / als alle Häringsfanger in gantz Engeland und Holand in tausend Jahren thun möchten; (*KJ,* pp. 75 f.)

Asaneth went home and estimated that that day she had caught more [fish] than all herring-fishers in England and Holland might catch in a thousand years.

The narration is then totally drawn into the author's present time when Grimmelshausen has Joseph distribute food, "gleichsam / wie man jetziger Zeit den Soldaten ihr Commißbrod gibt" (*KJ*, p. 121) ("in a similar way as nowadays one passes out the army bread to the soldiers")—a leap into the period of the Thirty Years' War. The author's liking for blunt, sometimes coarse language becomes obvious, when he says, for example, about Selicha, that she went

als wolte sie heimlich verrichten / worzu wir Menschen beyderley Geschlechts von Natur keine Zuseher zu begehren pflegen; das ist / sich etwas leichter zu machen: aber in Warheit / so hätte sie lieber eine Bürde auf sich genommen / welche just so schwer / als Joseph gewest wäre; worzu man zwar euch keine Zeugen erbittet; (*KJ*, pp. 42 f.)

as if she wanted to do secretly that for which we humans of either sex by nature do not like to have witnesses; that is, to make herself a bit lighter; but actually she would rather have carried a weight which was just as heavy as Joseph; something for which one also doesn't ask for witnesses;

Bluntness, proverbial sayings, and sensual or obscene metaphors and comparisons appear constantly and create a familiar atmosphere, as can only be found in the picaresque novels of Grimmelshausen and Beer. Simplicity and directness are the basic principles of this narration. The style is most adequate to the message: description of the triumph over the world by an exemplary man through his trust in God, a theme which would not at all be suitable for the gallant, courtly style.

VIII *Philipp von Zesen,* Assenat

The author's first original novel after the publication of *Die Adriatische Rosemund* (1645), Philipp von Zesen's Joseph novel *Assenat* was first published in 1670 in Amsterdam. In the meantime, Zesen had produced a variety of works: translations, lyrics, a treatise on poetics, historical works, devotional works, and much occasional and social literature in German, Latin, and Dutch. During the following years, *Assenat* was reprinted several times, once in 1672 and twice in 1679, and from 1711 to

1776 there appeared at least six editions in Danish translation. Thus, it can be considered Zesen's most successful novel.

In his preface Zesen makes it clear that he is not writing a story of his own invention but rather one based on three ancient sources, namely: (1) "im meisten [...] der Assenat Geschicht" ("mainly the story of Assenat"); (2) the "Verfassung des letzten Willens der zwölf Ertzväter" (the "last will of the twelve patriarchs"); and (3) "Schriften [...] des weltberühmten Atanasius Kirchers" ("Writings of the world-famous Atanasius Kircher"). The first source, the so-called *Historia Assenat*, is a story about Joseph's wife, with features of a saint's legend which was written in the spirit of Christian ideals. Besides the Old Testament,[45] it is very probably Zesen's most important source. The second title conceals a pseudoepigraphic book entitled *Testamente der Zwölf Patriarchen*, an imitation of Genesis 49, the blessing and prophecy of Jacob, in which Jacob's twelve sons, like their father, give their descendants final instructions while on their deathbeds. Among the works of the famous Jesuit scholar Atanasius Kircher (1601-80), Zesen has primarily used the *Oedipus Aegyptiacus*, which appeared in Rome in 1652-54. In this he found the greatest part of his archaeological, geographical, religious-historical, and linguistic-historical facts about Egypt and the Egyptians. In addition to these sources he used other more recent scholarly works, as well as sources from antiquity, such as Flavius Josephus, Herodotus, Diodorus, Strabo, Pliny, and Plutarch.

The number of writers from whom Zesen has drawn is tremendous, as the index of the modern reprint of *Assenat*, edited by Volker Meid, demonstrates (*A*, pp. 42* ff.). In addition to the index Zesen has added to this novel almost two hundred pages of notes ("Kurtzbündige Anmärckungen"), in which he both comments on his novel and documents it by quoting his sources. In his preface, he even recommends reading these notes first for a better understanding of the novel (*A*, p. [*A*, VIII^r]).[46] Obviously, Zesen has gone too far in this respect. But with *Assenat* the courtly-historical novel is first supplied with extensive scholarly notes at the conclusion which, although somewhat shorter, Lohenstein's *Arminius* was to list as well.

Whereas Grimmelshausen had consciously attempted to assimilate biblical history and Egyptian antiquity in the framework of his own age, Zesen attempts to lend his work Middle Eastern local color.[47] In so doing, he leaves the Jewish-Canaanite culture totally in the background, concentrating on the Egyptian culture without making use of the possibility of contrasting the two. He not only provides cultural-historical notes in the commentary at the end of the novel, but an entire series of instructive digressions are inserted into the text, satisfying the reader's interest in curiosities, strange customs, and the like. In *Die Adriatische Rosemund,* too, we find scholarly essays, but in *Assenat* they are not only shorter, they are also much better integrated into the novel. In many cases, they emanate directly from the action or are casually introduced into a conversation, following the model of Barclay's *Argenis.*[48] In the first book, for example, in a conversation between Josef and the chambermaid Semesse, an oracle which foretells Assenat's future is mentioned. In this oracle, the Nile is mentioned; consequently, Josef is given the opportunity to make detailed inquiries about this river, its springs, and its function with regard to the fertility of the land, in order to be better equipped to interpret the divine oracle. The Egyptian local color is given in diverting episodes as well; among them are descriptions of Egyptian gods and cultic festivities (*A,* pp. 1 f., 110, 130 ff.), pyramids and obelisks (*A,* pp. 208 ff., 233 ff.), and the description of the embalming of Assenat, which borders on the realm of tastelessness (*A,* pp. 306 ff.). The extraordinary, the strange, and the miraculous aspects of this world are underscored over and over. The scholarly digressions and notes render the work an approximation of the contemporary travelogues. Here Zesen does not present himself as the novelist who wants to entertain or preach morality, but rather as the seventeenth-century scholar who is interested in encyclopedic knowledge, and whose predilection for informative writings is imbued in the very texture of the novel. At the very least, he cannot be spared the reproach of affectation.

Assenat contains other elements of the courtly-historical novel as well. Zesen does not narrate in chronological order, as does Grimmelshausen in his *Keuscher Joseph,* but he begins *in medias res.* Josef is entering Memphis, riding on an elephant. His life up to this point, his having been sold by his brothers and the rest are told at a later point by a servant from Canaan. In addition,

Assenat shares with the courtly-historical novel the emphasis on courtly festivities and descriptions of the splendor connected with them. One festivity appears to follow the other, be it a religious observance or a wedding, which is celebrated with greatest pomp, with the detailed and meticulous description of all particulars—the parades, the customs, the clothes worn by the dignitaries, and so on. Zesen describes Josef's inauguration and his wedding in no less than fifty-nine pages, as compared to the five pages needed by Grimmelshausen.[49]

However, the novel, at the same time, contains an entire array of elements which distinguish it from the courtly-historical novel (as Zigler, Duke Anton Ulrich, and Lohenstein wrote it).[50] For instance, it has only one pair of lovers, namely Josef and Assenat. The fact that Zesen, in contrast to Grimmelshausen, has associated with Assenat—a rather passive character —an active comrade by the name of Nitokris, who aids Josef in prison and assists him in his release, does not help to increase the number of couples. When, at the conclusion, Nitokris marries the Libyan crown prince, the reader is left with the impression that Zesen wanted to eliminate her from the action in an elegant manner, as her presence is no longer required for the remainder of the work. Josef makes Assenat's acquaintance very late in the work. The Heliodoric scheme of meeting, separation, and reunification is, therefore, not realized. On the contrary, because of Nitokris' active aid, Josef and Assenat are brought together almost automatically, as they are finally united. The wedding does not take place at the end of the novel in a final apotheosis, but is the climax *within* the body of the novel. The action continues long afterward. The novel ends with the death of Josef, whom Zesen (with the aid of a farfetched etymology) makes into an Egyptian god. The action covers ninety-three years, since Josef's upbringing in Canaan (seventeen years) and part of Assenat's childhood (eight years) occur before the beginning of the narrative. That, too, is contrary to the principle of the courtly-historical novel—starting the action only a short time before the novel's conclusion and limiting it to approximately one year. Consequently, the recounting of what happened beforehand comprises only about thirty-five pages for both Josef's and Assenat's stories. There can be no consideration of any artificial scheme of confusion or of a knot which is untied at the conclusion of the work.

It has already been observed in Grimmelshausen's *Keuscher Joseph* that the goddess Fortuna had been excluded from the novel by Joseph's firm belief in God and the various kinds of prophecies, oracles, and dreams. Zesen, to be sure, seems to hold to the principle of the inconstancy of all worldly affairs rather superficially, as, for example, when he talks very generally about the inconstancy of time (A, p. 304) or when he repeatedly quotes fate itself ("das Verhängnüs") (A, pp. 77, 199). However, these instances merely represent the use of literary *topoi* which were fashionable during the seventeenth century. They are meaningless sayings rather than serious strong assertions of the Fortune idea. On the contrary, the use of dreams in Zesen's *Assenat* makes it evident how unavoidable the events of the novel are. The princess Nitokris, her servant Semesse, and Assenat herself have simultaneous dreams predicting Josef's and Assenat's fate. These dreams are interpreted with the help of the unsuspecting Josef, and Nitokris identifies Josef and Assenat as the dream figures. Nitokris therefore views the future as a fait accompli, and she actively tries to contribute to the fulfillment of these dreams. Grimmelshausen's Asaneth aids the enslaved Joseph, who has been thrown into prison, not only because she knows that he is innocent, but also because she loves him for his virtue. Zesen's Assenat, however, does not even know Josef because she grows up in the seclusion of a temple. Her girl friend Nitokris assists Josef because she sees him, through the dreams, as Assenat's future husband and the ruler of Egypt; her knowledge of his innocence is somewhat irrelevant. Nitokris knows the future, and she actively works for its realization. The net of dreams and oracles which encompasses the entire novel is much denser, much finer than that found in Grimmelshausen's *Keuscher Joseph*. By unnecessarily repeating the prophecies, Zesen has overused the dream motif to the point where it has become a playful game with arabesque motifs. However, in contrast to Grimmelshausen, astrology no longer has its magical character. It has found its place very reasonably in Zesen's belief in the benign government of heaven.[51] Consequently, Zesen feels compelled to state, in a theoretical discussion regarding dreams, that their fulfillment depends on the conduct of man. He interprets the stars as God's warning signals, so that He can reward man or punish him according to his behavior (*A*, pp. 149 f.). By thus indirectly reintroducing man's freedom of will, Zesen does not avoid the censure of contradicting himself—he previously had Nitokris act under the opposite assumption. De facto in *Assenat* the inconstant world of the courtly-historical novel which was ruled by Fortuna has given way to the structured, predetermined world in which the future has already been fixed by God.

Zesen does not title his novel after his main character Josef but rather after Assenat, a figure who remains rather pale and passive. He thus operates in the tradition of the great French and German courtly-historical novels, which bear the name of their heroine. The contrast to the title of Grimmelshausen's Joseph novel is significant. By calling his novel *Keuscher Joseph,* Grimmelshausen has already indicated that his work centers around a moral, ethical decision of his hero. In Zesen's novel as well, Josef, according to the sources, overcomes the temptation of Potiphar's wife. But this scene of temptation, so central in Grimmelshausen's novel, is not nearly as essential in Zesen's *Assenat.* The real center of *Assenat* is rather Josef's union with Assenat, that is, their wedding, and in connection with it, Josef's being raised to the position of the second most powerful man in Egypt. This shift of emphasis is already expressed in the subtitle of the novel; Zesen calls his work "Assenat; das ist Derselben / und des Josefs Heilige Stahts= Lieb= und Lebens-geschicht" ("Assenat; that is her and Josef's holy state, love and life story").

In his preface ("Dem Deutschgesinnten Leser"), he feels compelled to defend the adjective "heilig" in the title. He maintains rather arrogantly that he was writing about something new, foreign, exotic, and holy about which, in such a manner, no one had ever written (*A*, p. [A, Vʳ]). He calls his story holy, "weil sie aus dem brunnen der heiligen geschichte Göttlicher Schrift geflossen" (*A*, p. [A, Vʳ]) ("because it has flowed out of the well of the holy story of Divine Scripture"). The holy character is, moreover, underlined by the fact that Assenat has been educated by priests.[52] More important is the fact that Zesen calls his novel a story concerning state affairs, because his Josef conducts himself primarily as a statesman; the hero's family history is purposely relegated to the background. Josef himself points out that, through his suggested storage of food, the king's power and his splendor would be considerably increased (A, p. 173). During the numerous celebrations, he again and again speaks to the king about state affairs, and when the Libyan crown prince asks for the hand of princess Nitokris, he points out that the marriage would definitely be in the interest of the state (A, p. 261). Josef proves to be the circumspect representative of a patriarchal, yet absolutist, power state. Zesen thus fully adheres to the most popular political theories of the seventeenth century.[53] Josef even goes so far as to establish censorship offices before which each Egyptian must render account of his life in order to prevent general laziness during the seven fat years. The seven meager years Josef skillfully utilizes to increase the king's privileges and wealth as well as to enforce a new division of property, which redistributes the fields, leases the manors as fiefs, and determines the tax rates. Josef also proves himself to be a statesman by founding a university, in which mathematics, astrology, and other scholastic disciplines are taught (A, p. 297), and when in his more advanced age he has made enemies, he silences all who, out of envy, have criticized him by transforming a huge swamp area into fertile fields within an amazingly short time. The founding of cities is also mentioned (A, pp. 326 f.). Consequently, Zesen characterizes Josef as a model for all statesmen:

Josef war ein rechter Lehrspiegel vor alle Stahtsleute. Er gab ein lehrbild allen Beamten der Könige und Fürsten. Vor diesen edlen Spiegel möchten alle Stahtsleute / alle Amtsleute / alle Befehlshaber trähten / und sich bespiegeln. (A, p. 238)

Josef was a true model for all statesmen. He set an example for all officials of the kings and the princes. All statesmen, all officials, all commanders should step in front of this mirror and model themselves after him.

Just like Josef they would be rewarded by personal wealth for their just and virtuous behavior. Even on his deathbed Josef is concerned about the public weal, when he has his political testament handed over to the king seeking advice (A, p. 336). Thus, the courtly festivities are supplemented by Josef's political activity. Both elements relegate completely to the background the action concerning Josef and his family, that is, the family story as well as the action of his own moral conflict. It has been stated that *Assenat* does not entirely fit into the category of a courtly-historical novel. However, with its courtly elements and with its exemplary description of Josef as a statesman, it must be termed a novel of state affairs, a special type of the courtly-historical novel which was introduced by Barclay's *Argenis*.

The style of *Assenat*[54] is not characterized by a complicated structure or by diversified ornamentation, as would be expected, considering its content, but rather by syntactic brevity. Zesen himself calls such a style "lakonisch" ("laconic") or "kurtz-bündig" ("concise"). It is characteristic for *Assenat* that one and the same idea is usually repeated twice, sometimes once or three times, as, for example, when Josef reflects about his father's grief:

Ich war sein einiger trost. Ich war seine einige freude; der einige stab seines alters. Aber ach siehe! was hat er nun. Dieser stab ist ihm entrükket: diese freude ist ihm entzogen: dieser trost ist ihm geraubet. (A, p. 4)

I was his only consolation. I was his only joy; the only staff of his old age. But alas, hark! what does he have now. His staff is taken away from him: this joy has been withdrawn from him: this consolation has been stolen from him.

The short sentences here repeat the same idea in identical sequence of the parts of the sentence. This parallelism is used in *Assenat* quite frequently; only rarely we find the chiasmic reversal of the parts of the sentence.

The laconic style has various functions; its main purpose is to emphasize high points of the action and to maintain the level of style by varying repetition.[55] Too, the laconic style can assume the function of summarizing (e.g., A, p. 183). Laconic style is to be found on almost every page of *Assenat*. However, it is not appropriate for longer narrations; consequently, Zesen does not use it for his essaylike, scholarly insertions or when he simply describes action. Then he uses a terse, limited periodic style, which he calls "gemeine Mittelart" ("common middle way"), a style which, in contrast to long complex sentences, tends more to the staccato. Both types of style are frequently used together;

one type is infused into the other, creating a merging of the two.[56]

The Joseph theme was treated once again in the novelistic literature of the seventeenth century: In 1697 the novel *Assenath* by Joachim Meier (1661-1732) appeared. He was the director of the *Gymnasium* in Göttingen, and wrote a total of five biblical novels.[57] Joseph is now the hero of only one of four episodes. He has been raised to the level of a Hebrew prince, who now, according to the Heliodoric structure of the courtly-historical novel (which is very mechanically implemented), pursues his abducted bride. He proves himself a hero by defeating thieves and by corralling a stampeding herd of horses. Sephira has become a scheming intrigante, who, in the end, is exposed before the entire court. The contrast to Zesen's version is obvious; in *Assenat* Sephira's guilt is not even made public after her death. In Meier's novel God's providence is also lacking—in its place we encounter once more the inconstant goddess Fortuna of the courtly-historical novel. The Joseph story is here merely the subject of a courtly-historical novel, which has been constructed according to the popular recipe, excluding the moral concepts of the philosophy of life of a writer such as Grimmelshausen or Zesen which were visible even through the abundance of traditional, mechanically used, popular motifs.

IX   *The Gallant Novel*
Christian Friedrich Hunold: Die liebenswürdige Adalie

Just in time for the Easter book fair in the year 1706, the publisher Benjamin Wedel from Hamburg published a novel entitled *Satyrischer* ROMAN, *In Unterschiedlichen / lustigen / lächerlichen und galanten Liebes=Begebenheiten.* von Menantes. Menantes was the pen name of Christian Friedrich Hunold, who had used for this novel scandalous occurrences of the Hamburg society. The appearance of the novel caused a tremendous arousal of public feeling. The municipal judge of Hamburg ordered immediate confiscation of the book; and the author as well as the publisher were sued for slander by distinguished and influential citizens. "Ein gewisser teutscher Fürst" ("a certain German prince") sent out a number of dragoons to search for the author, and in Leipzig there was even a rumor that a reward of fifty talers had been offered for Hunold's arrest. Hunold felt his life to be in jeopardy, so one night he left the town under the cover of darkness.

Christian Friedrich Hunold[58] was born September 29, 1781, in Wandersleben, a Thuringian village in the vicinity of Arnstadt. Having been orphaned in early childhood, he attended elementary school in Arnstadt and the *Gymnasium* in Weißenfels. At the age of eighteen he began to study law at the University of Jena, in addition to languages, rhetorics, and poetry. His teacher was August Bohse, who had made a name as a successful novelist, writing under the pseudonym *Talander*.[59] Bohse was Hunold's model in his own later literary endeavors. Hunold lived the life of a young cavalier: he learned fencing and dancing and enjoyed great popularity with the young ladies. It is no wonder that he one day discovered that his paternal estate had dwindled to nothing. Hunold seems to have lost his reason over this state of affairs, and at the beginning of the year 1700 he went to Hamburg.

Hamburg was the right place for a young half-academic adventurer: it was a city of 150,000 inhabitants in which world-wide commerce had also brought about a tremendous development of cultural activities. Most prosperous was the Hamburg opera, which had been founded in 1678 and which offered musicians and poets the chance to work and be productive.

Since Hunold could not find an appropriate job, he soon attempted to become a writer. Within a few years he wrote four voluminous novels, several volumes of poems, two opera libretti, treatises on poetics, guides for letter writing, books on public decorum and etiquette, a comedy, and several translations from French literature (La Fontaine). His situation explains why Hunold started to write: he was not driven by an inner compulsion but rather by the necessity of making a living. Writing novels seemed to be the easiest way to accomplish this. Driven away from Hamburg on account of the scandal over the *Satyrischer Roman,* he finally found employment in Halle by obtaining a doctorate and delivering lectures on ethics, German rhetorics, and poetry. The former *enfant terrible* of society had become a respected citizen and a professor. It is not surprising that his publications from this period are pious and somewhat monotonous. Hunold died in 1721 at the age of forty.

Besides the *Satyrischer Roman,* Hunold wrote three other novels, all of which were published in numerous editions, which demonstrated their extensive popularity. Hunold's novels have been classified as gallant novels.[60] *Die liebens⹀Würdige Adalie,* Hamburg, 1702 (and later 1714, 1731, 1752) shall be used to demonstrate what distinguishes a so-called gallant novel from a work of the courtly-historical genre:

The German prince Rosantes, who is incognito in Paris as the son of a merchant Bosardo from Elbipolis (Hamburg), falls in love with Adalie, the sweet and attractive daughter of the merchant Brion. Due to the fact that a war is threatening to break out between Germany and France, Rosantes flees to England, supposedly in order to return from there to Elbipolis. Adalie goes to Germany as the companion of a duchess. At the court of Allerona she sees the sleeping Rosantes, thinks he is a ghost, and flees. In Elbipolis she finds Bosardo's real son to be a young dandy instead of her beloved Rosantes, and she flees with her maid Doris to the latter's home in a neighboring area. She is invited to the castle of Princess Emilie, where Count Alfredo, who had been previously courting Emilie, proposes marriage to Adalie in order to escape a rejection by Emilie, who has hopes of catching Rosantes. Adalie agrees, somewhat reluctantly, in the belief that Rosantes is dead. One hour after the agreement Rosantes arrives. After a short duel, Alfredo agrees to give up his claims to Adalie: he marries Emilie, whereas Rosantes and Adalie marry in Allerona.

Parallel to this main action is a supporting action. Renard, a cavalier who has been rejected by Adalie, is accepted as the husband-to-be by her sister Barsine, who is living in a monastery. But Barsine is abducted by Lionard, who is killed by Renard in pursuit. However, Barsine disappears. Continuing his search, Renard comes to a castle, invited by a lady by the name of Arminde. Louyse, the lady of the castle, is giving a party. She has also invited Bellardo, Arminde's wooer, against the latter's will. During the course of the evening, Louyse offers to pay Renard a nocturnal visit in his room. Renard obtains the same favor from Arminde. At Louyse's request the rejected Bellardo acts as a substitute. The following morning Louyse does not know that she has disported with Renard's chamberlain, whereas Arminde accepts Bellardo.

Searching farther, Renard finally finds Barsine, who is held prisoner by the wicked Curton in his castle. Rosantes comes as her liberator, and Curton is told of his death sentence, which is not meant to be enforced. By experiencing fear of death he is "morally bettered."

The Cinderella-like rise of a merchant's daughter to a duchess was the novelistic theme which was unprecedented in Hunold's time, because, until this point, the courtly-historical novels had only had princes and princesses as their heroes and heroines. Such a rise in social status was in diametrical contrast to all social ethics of the time. The burgher classes were very concerned about preserving their circles intact and allowed no intermarriages with lower classes. How much more so the nobility with all its fine differences in rank and birth! This is often difficult for a man of the twentieth century to comprehend. But toward the end of the seventeenth century, the social system had started to shift and weaken; the limits of the social classes were loosened. The favorites of the princes were ennobled; electors became kings, and ruling counts became princes. The princes added new positions to their courts, and the Viennese court chancery was only too eager to bestow honors and titles for money or political advantage. However, whereas a man had the chance to advance in a career at court, a woman could arrive socially only by marriage. But the realization of such a young girl's dream is the more sensational, since marrying a prince, without oneself belonging to the high nobility, was still, at this point, a Cinderella fairy tale.

What had actually happened was this: Duke Georg Wilhelm of Luneburg-Celle had married the beautiful and intelligent French girl Eléonore d'Olbreuse (1638-1725), the daughter of a poor country nobleman from Poitou, that is, the daughter of a member of the low nobility had become a ruling duchess.[61] This subject was soon taken up by the French scandal literature. In 1679 an anonymous report of these events appeared in Paris, and during the same year the subject was turned into an entertaining little novel called *L'Illustre Parisienne* by Sieur Jean de Préchac. Préchac changes the girl of poor nobility into the daughter of a Parisian banker, with whom the German prince, traveling incognito, falls in love. Préchac's novel contains the main action of Hunold's *Adalie*; Hunold has simply translated, paraphrased, added individual scenes, and included, primarily, the Renard/Barsine-action. Consequently, it is no accident that this subplot contains chiefly those elements which constitute the so-called gallant novel. The question now must be posed: What in *Adalie,* taken as an example of the gallant novel, is at variance with the courtly-historical novel?

(1) The action takes place in a socially lower class. Rosantes is a prince, but Adalie is the daughter of a merchant—a burgher. The Hamburg merchant Bosardo also fills an important role. Most of the other persons as well do not belong to the high nobility; the majority of them are members of the landed gentry (Renard, Curton) or city patricians. On the whole, a lower social stratum is depicted.

(2) The consequence of the shift in social emphasis is that *private* love affairs play a central role instead of important political events or love affairs which can determine the fate of states. Princes and lovers are not identical. No wars are waged for the beloved girl. Political events are, for the most part, in the background; they occasionally separate the lovers but have no power or political influence of their own. The gallant novel is nonpolitical and is personality oriented.

(3) The action takes place at well-known locales, either precisely named or anagrammatically circumscribed, during the author's present time. The author of a gallant novel does not delve into Germanic or Roman antiquity. There is no trace of the emphasis on exotic elements, as is found in Zigler, Zesen, and Duke Anton Ulrich.

(4) In the courtly-historical novel, the hero distinguishes himself by unparalleled bravery, annihilating entire armies; for example, contrast Hunold's Rosantes, who immediately flees to England, when he is in danger of being arrested without even visiting his beloved Adalie beforehand. Renard succeeds in killing Lionard, but he is still unable to overcome Curton on his own. The hero of a gallant novel is not required to possess extraordinary bravery, but only a good education, since around the turn of the century the ideal of the time had changed. A man was no longer required simply to possess personal bravery and intelligence; he had also to be a *galanthomme* and to possess a social *conduite* as it was practiced at the courts, which in turn

faithfully imitated the French customs. In the gallant novel the courtly-historical novel is "domesticated."

(5) A mastering of the rules of etiquette is a manifestation of the emphasis on good education. Prince Rosantes has traveled to Paris in order to acquire the mastery of the forms of behavior which were considered so essential. He and Renard are those who master the rules of proper conduct, whereas Curton as well as the Count Alfredo often do not display seemly behavior. The period of the high point of the gallant novel was also a time in which books teaching proper behavior and guides for letter writing were published en masse. It is not accidental that Bohse (Talander) and Hunold are at the same time authors of such works. To a certain extent, the gallant novel is also a book of manners and a guide for letter writing. The numerous compliments of the heroes to their ladies are model compliments written in order to be memorized as patterns. The letters are model letters, which often have no relationship whatsoever to the action. The didactic tendency of the gallant novel represents a complete shift into the area of socially correct behavior. Factual knowledge, encyclopedic and essayistic insertions, as were found in the novels of Lohenstein, Zesen, or Eberhard Werner Happel (1647-90), are all missing in Hunold's gallant novels.

(6) New to the gallant novel is its ethos. In the courtly-historical novel, the separation of the hero and the heroine was a means of proving their ethical qualities; it was a test of their constancy and fidelity to each other. The hero is protected by Divine Providence which does not allow his defeat nor the heroine's despair, although she has to believe her lover to be dead. When Adalie believes Rosantes to have died, she gives way to elegiac moods in a bucolic environment, but can also be readily persuaded to accept Alfredo's marriage proposal, confessing that she loves Alfredo, although she obviously loved Rosantes more than him. Where in the courtly-historical novel is there such a variance in the degrees of love? The partners are changed again just as quickly when it turns out that Rosantes is still alive. All are amazed that Alfredo does not immediately retrench but wants to fight for his fiancée. Finally, an agreement is achieved over a good breakfast! The standards of the gallant novel are no longer absolute; they are no longer based on a Divine foundation. Only the virtue of adapting to the given

conditions, the virtue of conciliation, is considered valuable. Society is absolutizing itself, taking the place of the Divine order and setting its own standards. Belonging to, and being accepted by, society is the highest value. An ethical order of the world outside society does not exist.

(7) The old Heliodoric scheme of the late Greek and the courtly-historical novel is maintained. In *Adalie* there are two couples who meet, are separated, are united again, and marry (Rosantes/Adalie; Renard/Barsine). In comparison to Duke Anton Ulrich's novels, two couples represent a tremendous simplification. The number of characters has been reduced in comparison to what is found in the courtly-historical novel. Correspondingly smaller is the number of pages: five hundred small pages, mostly in octavo format, is the most that these novels consist of (*Adalie* boasts 461 pages). Thus, the gallant novel, with regard to size and number of characters, is a somewhat shrunken version of the courtly-historical novel. The happy end with the wedding of the lovers is still obligatory, but is no longer the reward for exemplary conduct as is the case in the courtly-historical novel.

(8) The composition is often very loose. Numerous short forms have been inserted into the novel, so that the main action is frequently skeletal. When the author returns to the action, the reader in many cases has to think for a minute in order to recall the previous situation, when the thread of the action was dropped. The joke, the amusing merry-tale-like insertion, the often silly prank played on someone is the most preferred of these inserted forms, because the result is that someone is being laughed at. Again and again comical situations are described which deal with the harmless intrigues, mistaken identities, and situations which do not threaten or harm any of the characters.

(9) Probably the best example for the motif of intrigue is Renard's stay at the castle while he is searching for Barsine. This scene, like many others, serves the sole purpose of entertaining the reader, having no results or consequences within the framework of the novel. For this reason, Herbert Singer has termed the gallant novel in its purest form a *Komödienroman* (comedy-novel),[62] as the courtly-historical novel may be compared to the tragedy in the field of drama. Thus, the loss of tragic seriousness has been recognized as an essential element

of Hunold's novels, the loss of a model character who serves to set standards, the dissolution into a meaningless, insignificant game.

(10) Another factor is demonstrated by this episode in the castle: With the loss of traditional ideals a new interpretation of the world has taken their place. The world is a showcase of love into which the reader gains insight as a secret observer. The true hero in such a world is the sly and cunning *Amor*, who steals into the heart, causing persons such as Louyse or Arminde to become unfaithful, and implicating Renard in the frivolous game—at least to the point at which he can barely maintain his faithfulness to Barsine. It is the play with seduction, frivolity, levity, and restriction of the themes to jokes, gallant love, and social life, all of which elements are found again in the lyrics of the literary Rococo in the eighteenth century. This leads to the conclusion that the gallant novel is actually the novel of early Rococo.[63]

The lack of norms and the insertion of forms foreign to the genre point up a general confusion of the generic criteria in the German novel around 1700. A general syncretism of genres begins. The intrusion of the joke, the merry tale, marks this development in Hunold. Novels of the kind which, for example, Johann Beer wrote—in the final analysis eclectic products of the picaresque novel—come surprisingly close to the gallant novel. The ethos and the series of motifs employed are almost identical, and the inserted merry tales also resemble each other. Just as in Beer's novels religious elements are present, as represented by the hermit scenes, in Hunold's novels the characters form, temporarily, a sort of pietistic conventicle, as, for example, in the case of the "conversion" of the sinner Curton. Just as in Beer's novels the *picaro* is often a mere observer, and the nobleman takes on the role of the *picaro*, in Hunold's novels, too, the "heroes" of the pranks are the same country noblemen, so that Beer could justifiably be placed into the group of authors of the gallant novel (Bohse, Hunold) as well as into a class with Grimmelshausen.

The gallant novel was introduced by Bohse and perfected by Hunold, but the type was not popular for long. The syncretism of the genres, the lack of generally accepted ethical norms, the experimenting of writers at the end of an old and the beginning of a new era prevented a codification of genre requirements, especially since most literary theoreticians did not yet acknowledge the novel as a separate genre, considering the writing of novels—and above all a gallant novel—a kind of juvenile prank on the part of the author, serving two purposes only: providing the writer with income while entertaining the readers.

Among Hunold's followers, the following may be mentioned: the Nuremberg patrician and scholar Johann Leonhard Rost (1688-1727), author of discourses on astronomy, translations, and at least nine novels, which he composed according to Bohse's and Hunold's delineations under the pseudonym *Meletaon*, and Melissus, a pseudonym, which probably represents the doctor Otto Philipp Virdung von Hartung from Bamberg. His novel *Des glückseligen Ritters Adelphico Lebens= und Glücks= Fälle* (1715) closely resembles Hunold's creations. The gallant novel also experienced a late flowering in Johann Gottfried Schnabel's *Der im Irrgarten der Liebe herumtaumelnde Kavalier* (1746).[64] Schnabel is today much better known for his robinsonade *Die Insel Felsenburg* (4 vols., 1731-43),[65] a novel which is written entirely in the spirit of the eighteenth century. Since 1720 the gallant novel has had few if any representatives. With its artificial late realization, the age of the Baroque came to an end.

CHAPTER 4

Conclusion

THE situation regarding the German novel during the first decades of the eighteenth century is a much more confusing one than was the case during the seventeenth century. As has been previously indicated, around 1700 the greatest number of heterogeneous elements had found their way into the traditional types of the novel. Foreign genres had claimed the title of novels: satires, scandal novels, biographies, books of devotion, pasquinades, and so on. A general dissolution, a syncretism of the genres was the logical consequence.

But what influence did the types of the novel which were popular during the seventeenth century have on those of the eighteenth century? How long did these seventeenth-century genres stay alive? Were the earlier genres transformed into new ones? Around 1720 the political novel was "on its last legs," and the pastoral novel was practically dead. Its bucolic world, however, was to live on in the lyrics of the Anacreontics and in the pastoral idylls of the second half of the eighteenth century. The majority of the novels from the first decades of the eighteenth century are decadent epigonal courtly-historical novels, which, in this latter form, led an anachronistic but long-lasting life until the middle of the century. Over and over the heroes leave their homeland in order to free their beloved girls from the hands of their abductors; they fight against robbers, are shipwrecked, disguise themselves, and so on, thus very mechanically fulfilling the Heliodoric scheme without believing in the underlying philosophy of the anonymous fate. The writers mask themselves behind pseudonyms; no great novels like those by Lohenstein or Duke Anton Ulrich appear on the scene.

The picaresque novel, with Johann Beer, on the one hand, and the political novel, on the other, in its final stage was to find various successors during the eighteenth century:

(1) A number of novels were published in which the action takes place among students in university cities, using this setting as a license for amorous episodes and promiscuity. The titles serve to characterize these novels: Celander, *Der Verliebte Studente*, 1709; Sarcander, *Amor auf Universitäten*, 1710; Florindus, *Betrüglicher Courtesie-Spiegel Des Academischen Frauenzimmers*, 1714; Incognitus, *Der verliebte und galante Student*, 1734. Since in these books primarily erotic episodes and anecdotes are related, and since an overall structure which holds the whole together is often hardly recognizable, or seems artificially appended, these works can hardly be regarded as novels.[1]

(2) The publication of Daniel Defoe's *Robinson Crusoe* (1719) triggered the appearance of a whole wave of German robinsonades. Not all novels (which had the word *Robinsonade* in their title) were actually robinsonades; they were often simply adventure novels, tales of distant travels and romantic adventures.[2] It hardly needs to be mentioned that almost every German province had its representative Robinson; there was a Saxon, a Swiss, a Bohemian, a Frisian, a Jutish, and, even a female Robinson! The best known and most highly acclaimed example of this group is Johann Gottfried Schnabel's *Insel Felsenburg* (4 vols., 1731/43).

At the end of the 1730's and in the early 1740's, a new type of novel was gaining ground in Germany, which has recently been characterized as a novel with a moral tendency (*moralischer Tendenzroman*).[3] It is distinguished by its moralistic attitude, by inserting moralistic essays; and, in order to exert a positive ethical influence on the reader, it presents the life history or histories of morally exemplary persons or of persons who, because of their vices, are meant to have a deterrent effect on the reader. Betterment of the reader's moral attitude became the purpose in a time in which the moral weeklies, imported from England, began their triumphant career in Germany and when, at the same time, the movement of Pietism gained more and more followers. With the appearance of this type of novel, the best known representative of which is Christian Fürchtegott Gellert's *Das Leben der schwedischen Gräfin von G.* (2 vols., 1747/48), and later with the publication of Christoph Martin Wieland's *Die Geschichte des Agathon* (2 vols., 1766/67), new types of the novel established themselves, which were the products of the new bourgeois and individualistic world of the eighteenth century. By this time the age of the Thirty Years' War and the courtly culture was long dead and, with it, its novels.

Notes and References

Preface

1. Arnold Hirsch, "Barockroman und Aufklärungsroman," *Etudes Germaniques*, IX (1954), 7.

2. K. G. Knight, *Deutsche Romane der Barockzeit* (London, Methuen, 1969), p. 7.

3. Concerning Opitz' remarks about the epic, see Günther Müller, "Barockromane und Barockroman," *Literaturwissenschaftliches Jahrbuch der Görres-Gesellschaft*, IV (1929), pp. 9 f.; see also Dieter Kimpel and Conrad Wiedemann (eds.), *Theorie und Technik des Romans im 17. und 18. Jahrhundert*. Vol. I: "Barock und Aufklärung" (Tübingen: Max Niemeyer, 1971).

4. Herbert Singer, *Der galante Roman* (Stuttgart: Metzler, 1961), p. 10.

5. *Die bedeutendsten deutschen Romane des siebzehnten Jahrhunderts* (Leipzig, 1866; reprint: Darmstadt: Wissenschaftliche Buchgesellschaft, 1965).

6. Vol. I (Leipzig: Weber, 1926).

7. "Der deutsche Roman von der Renaissance bis zu Goethes Tod," *Deutsche Philologie im Aufriß*, ed. Wolfgang Stammler. Vol. II (Berlin, Bielefeld: Erich Schmidt, 1960), cols. 1217-1356.

8. "Der Roman des Barock," in: Hans Steffen (ed.) *Formkräfte der deutschen Dichtung vom Barock bis zur Gegenwart* (Göttingen: Vandenhoek & Ruprecht, 2nd. ed., 1967), pp. 21-34.

9. André Jolles, "Die literarischen Travestien Ritter-Hirt-Schelm," *Pikarische Welt: Schriften zum Europäischen Schelmenroman*, ed. Helmut Heidenreich. Wege der Forschung, Vol. 163 (Darmstadt: Wissenschaftliche Buchgesellschaft, 1969), pp. 101-18.

Chapter One

1. This distinction goes back to Heinrich Meyer, *Der deutsche Schäferroman des 17. Jahrhunderts* (Diss. Freiburg i.Br., 1927; published: Dorpat, 1928); see also the article "Schäferroman" by Heinrich Meyer, in: Paul Merker and Wolfgang Stammler (eds.), *Reallexikon der deutschen Literaturgeschichte*. Vol. III (Berlin: Walter de Gruyter, 1928/29), pp. 151-54.

2. This interpretation follows Peter Rusterholz, *Nachwort* to:

Martin Opitz, *Schäfferey von der Nimfen Hercinie*. Reclams Universal-Bibliothek, Vol. 8594 (Stuttgart, Reclam, 1969), pp. 71-79.

3. For further titles, plot summaries, and interpretations see Heinrich Meyer's dissertation (cf. note 1).

4. The only exception is Johann Thomas' *Damon und Lisille*.

5. See Arnold Hirsch, *Bürgertum und Barock im deutschen Roman*. 2nd edition, ed. Herbert Singer. Literatur und Leben, N.F. Vol. 1 (Köln, Graz: Böhlau, 1957), p. 93.

6. Meyer, *Der deutsche Schäferroman*, p. 107.

7. Paul Hankamer, *Deutsche Gegenreformation und deutsches Barock: Die deutsche Literatur im Zeitraum des 17. Jahrhunderts* (Stuttgart: Metzler, 3rd. ed., 1964), p. 401.

8. 1663 (two editions) and 1667. The 1667 edition contains a second part which consists of an anthology of lyrics by the author, primarily celebrating Lisille. Herbert Singer analyzes the novel in his *Nachwort* of *DL*. See also Hirsch, *Bürgertum*, pp. 104 f.

9. See Herbert Singer, *Nachwort* to *DL*, p. 238.

10. Klaus Kaczerowsky, *Bürgerliche Romankunst im Zeitalter des Barock: Philipp von Zesens "Adriatische Rosemund"* (Munich: Wilhelm Fink, 1969), pp. 7 f.

11. Karl Dissel, *Philipp von Zesen und die Deutschgesinnte Genossenschaft* (Hamburg: Programm des Wilhelm-Gymnasiums, 1890). Idem, "Philipp von Zesen," in *Allgemeine Deutsche Biographie*. Vol. 45 (Leipzig: Duncker & Humblot, 1900), pp. 108-18.

12. See Kaczerowsky, pp. 49 ff. Kaczerowsky has succeeded in reconciling all discrepancies between Zesen's biography and his novel.

13. Zesen was familiar with the courtly-historical novel through his translation of Mlle de Scudéry's *Ibrahim* (1641), which he published in 1645, even before *Die Adriatische Rosemund* appeared.

14. Comp. below, p. 107.

15. This also applies to the individualistic poetry of the seventeenth century. See Hans Obermann, *Studien über Philipp Zesens Romane* (Diss. Göttingen, 1933), p. 52.

16. See Obermann, p. 49.

17. See Kaczerowsky, pp. 120 ff.

18. See Obermann, p. 48 and Hans Körnchen, *Zesens Romane: Ein Beitrag zur Geschichte des Romans im 17. Jahrhundert*. Palaestra, Vol. 115 (Berlin: Mayer & Müller, 1912), pp. 93 ff.

20. This is Kaczerowsky's contention (p. 126), who makes this concept of *Die Adriatische Rosemund* the basis of his criticism of the Baroque as antithetical and courtly in spirit.

21. See Jan Hendrik Scholte, "Zesens 'Adriatische Rosemund,'" *DVJs.* XXIII (1949), 295.

22. Concerning the following, see Kaczerowsky, pp. 134 ff.

23. Translating foreign words into German was one of the main

tasks of German seventeenth-century poets who wished to create a German literary language which could compete with the foreign literatures.

24. See Körnchen, p. 103.

Chapter Two

1. See Adam Schneider, *Spaniens Anteil an der Deutschen Litteratur des 16. und 17. Jahrhunderts* (Straßburg: Schlesier & Schweikhardt, 1898), pp. 213 f.

2. This classification has been suggested by Werner Beck, *Die Anfänge des deutschen Schelmenromans: Studien zur frühbarocken Erzählung*. Zürcher Beiträge zur vergleichenden Literaturgeschichte, Vol. 8 (Zurich: Juris, 1957), p. 17.

3. It cannot be denied that there are substantial differences between the Renaissance novel *Lazarillo* and the later picaresque novels, which influenced Grimmelshausen's *Simplicissimus*. These differences, however, are irrelevant for the demonstration of the genre criteria.

4. The best enumeration of genre criteria is to be found in: Claudio Guillén, "Zur Frage der Begriffsbestimmung des Pikaresken," in: *Pikarische Welt*, ed. Helmut Heidenreich, pp. 375-96; see also Alewyn, "Der Roman des Barock," pp. 23 ff.

5. The difference between the German trickster of the sixteenth century and the *picaro* is the fact that the *picaro* fights for his physical survival and, therefore, must resort to tricks, whereas the trickster plays pranks for his own amusement.

6. See Jan Hendrik Scholte, *Der Simplicissimus und sein Dichter* (Tübingen: Niemeyer, 1950), pp. 7 f. Because of a separate TWAS volume on Grimmelshausen, my discussion of this author has been limited here.

7. Günther Weydt, "Zur Entstehung barocker Erzählkunst bei Harsdörffer und Grimmelshausen," *WW*, *Sonderheft*, I (1952), 61-72; also in: Günther Weydt (ed.), *Der Simplicissimusdichter und sein Werk*. Wege der Forschung, Vol. 153 (Darmstadt: Wissenschaftliche Buchgesellschaft, 1969), pp. 351-69.

8. See Artur Bechtold, "Zur Quellengeschichte des Simplicissimus," *Euphorion*, XIX (1912), 19-66 and 491-546.

9. Manfred Koschlig, "Das Lob des 'Francion' bei Grimmelshausen," *Jahrbuch der deutschen Schillergesellschaft*, I (1957), 30-73.

10. See Carl August von Bloedau, *Grimmelshausens Simplicissimus und seine Vorgänger*. Palaestra, Vol. 51 (Berlin: Mayer & Müller, 1908), p. 68.

11. Von Bloedau, p. 63, calls ST the first German historical novel; however, see Borcherdt, pp. 166 f.

12. Friedrich Gundolf, "Grimmelshausen und der Simplicissimus," *DVJs.*, I (1923), pp. 339-58; reprinted in: Weydt, *Der Simplicissimus-dichter*, pp. 111-32.

13. Scholte, *Der Simplicissimus und sein Dichter*, pp. 12 ff.

14. Grimmelshausen, *Simplicissimus Teutsch*, ed. Jan Hendrik Scholte, Neudrucke deutscher Literaturwerke des 16. und 17. Jahrhunderts, No. 302-9 (Tübingen: Max Niemeyer, 3rd. ed., 1954).

15. Also: Julius Petersen and Friedrich Streller. Cf. Alt see Weydt, *Der Simplicissimusdichter*, pp. 179 ff.

16. The following criticism is according to Günther Weydt, "Planetensymbolik im barocken Roman," *Doitsu Bungaku* [Die deutsche Literatur], XXXVI (1966), 1-14; reprinted in: Weydt, *Der Simplicissimusdichter*, pp. 266-81.

17. See Werner Welzig, *Beispielhafte Figuren: Tor, Abenteurer und Einsiedler bei Grimmelshausen* (Graz, Cologne: Hermann Böhlaus Nachf., 1963).

18. Clemens Lugowski, "Literarische Formen und lebendiger Gehalt im 'Simplicissimus,'" *Zeitschrift für Deutschkunde*, XLVIII (1948), 622-34; reprinted in: Weydt, *Der Simplicissimusdichter*, pp. 161-78.

19. The modern development novel often contains similar situations, for example, Hans Castorp between Settembrini and Naphta in Thomas Mann's *Zauberberg*.

20. Günther Rohrbach, *Figur und Charakter: Strukturuntersuchungen an Grimmelshausens Simplicissimus*. Bonner Arbeiten zur deutschen Literatur, Vol. 3 (Bonn: H. Bouvier & Co., 1959), p. 77; also in: Weydt, *Der Simplicissimusdichter*, p. 261.

21. Werner Hoffmann, "Grimmelshausens 'Simplicissimus'—Nicht doch ein Bildungsroman?" *GRM*, N.F. XVII (1967), 175.

22. Clemens Heselhaus interprets *ST* as a satirical novel in: "Grimmelshausen, *Der abenteuerliche Simplicissimus*," in: Benno von Wiese (ed.), *Der deutsche Roman: Vom Barock bis zur Gegenwart*, Vol. I (Düsseldorf: August Bagel, 1963), pp. 15-63. However, I cannot agree with Heselhaus' interpretation of the *Continuatio*, in which Heselhaus sees Simplicius as a *heiliger Schalk* ("holy rogue"), thus overlooking the serious attitude of Grimmelshausen, the moralist.

23. Concerning the Utopias, see Melitta Gerhard, *Der deutsche Entwicklungsroman bis zu Goethes "Wilhelm Meister"* (Bern: Francke, 2nd. ed., 1968), pp. 75 ff.; also in: Weydt, *Der Simplicissimusdichter*, pp. 148 ff.

24. Parallels to Wolfram von Eschenbach's medieval epic *Parzival* are obvious; they have been repeatedly pointed out, e.g., by Melitta Gerhard, pp. 62 ff.

25. Concerning the discussion of the *Continuatio* as a sequel written for commercial or other pertinent reasons, see Scholte, *Der*

Simplicissimus und sein Dichter, pp. 48 ff. and Helmut K. Krausse, "Das sechste Buch des Simplicissimus,—Fortsetzung oder Schluß?" *Seminar,* VI (1968), 129-46. For the allegorical significance see Siegfried Streller, *Grimmelshausens Simplicianische Schriften: Allegorie, Zahl und Wirklichkeitsdarstellung,* Neue Beiträge zur Literaturwissenschaft, Vol. 7 (Berlin: Rütten & Loening, 1957), pp. 40 ff.

26. Scholte, *Der Simplicissimus und sein Dichter,* pp. 49 ff.

27. See Heselhaus, pp. 57 f.

28. Richard Alewyn, *Johann Beer: Studien zum Roman des 17. Jahrhunderts,* Palaestra, Vol. 181 (Leipzig: Mayer & Müller, 1932).

29. Regarding Grimmelshausen's influence on Beer, see Alewyn, *Johann Beer,* pp. 158 ff.

30. See Alewyn, *Johann Beer,* p. 137 and Manfred Kremer, *Die Satire bei Johann Beer* (Diss., Cologne, 1954), p. 151.

31. Cf. Alewyn's interpretative essay in *JJ,* p. 147.

32. Alewyn, *Johann Beer,* p. 241.

33. In accordance with Manfred Kremer, pp. 122 ff. I do not consider it suitable to call Grimmelshausen a naturalist or Beer a realist, as Alewyn does.

34. Jörg-Jochen Müller, *Studien zu den Willenhag-Romanen Johann Beers.* Marburger Beiträge zur Germanistik, Vol. 9 (Marburg: N. G. Elwert, 1965), p. 62.

35. I cannot agree with Müller's thesis (p. 66) that Beer has created merely a literary landscape.

36. See Müller, p. 71.

37. See Alewyn, *Johann Beer,* p. 168.

38. See *ibid.,* p. 189.

39. *KS,* pp. 11 ff. and pp. 400 ff. Cf. Müller, p. 143.

40. See Müller, p. 104.

41. See Kremer, p. 154.

42. Friedrich Zarncke, *Christian Reuter, der Verfasser des Schelmuffsky: Sein Leben und seine Werke* (Leipzig: Hirzel, 1884), p. 467.

43. Concerning the difference between A and B, see Karl Tober, "Christian Reuters Schelmuffsky," *Zeitschrift für deutsche Philologie,* LXXXIV (1955), 127-50.

44. *Ibid.,* p. 135.

45. Joseph Risse's view that *Schelmuffsky* is primarily a *pasquillo* is today generally considered obsolete. See Risse, *Christian Reuters "Schelmuffsky" und sein Einfluß auf die deutsche Dichtung* (Diss., Münster, 1911), pp. 13 ff.

46. This is the often repeated opinion of Friedrich Zarncke (p. 512), which does apply to version A, but only in part to B.

47. Wolfgang Hecht, "Die Idee in Christian Reuters *Schelmuffsky,*" *Forschungen und Fortschritte,* XXIX (1955), 381-82 and idem,

Christian Reuter. Sammlung Metzler, Vol. 46 (Stuttgart: J. B. Metzler, 1966), pp. 38 f.

48. Hecht, *Christian Reuter,* p. 39.

49. Tober, p. 142.

50. Cf. Hans König, "Reuters Schelmuffsky als Typ der barocken Bramarbas-Dichtung" (Diss., Hamburg, 1945) and Hecht, *Christian Reuter,* p. 34.

51. Concerning the relation of *Schelmuffsky* to the picaresque novel, see Hecht, *Christian Reuter,* pp. 34 f. and Risse, pp. 33 ff.

52. Hecht, *Christian Reuter,* p. 35.

53. Concerning the influence of *Schelmuffsky* on later authors, see Risse, pp. 39 ff. (highly exaggerated), Hecht, *Christian Reuter,* pp. 60 ff. and Otto Deneke, *Schelmuffsky.* Göttingische Nebenstunden, Vol. 3 (Göttingen, published by the author/editor, 1927), pp. 17 ff.

54. See Deneke, *loc. cit.*

55. 1809, pp. 322-48.

56. As quoted by Hecht, *Christian Reuter,* p. 62.

57. See Rudolf Becker, *Christian Weises Romane und ihre Nachwirkung* (Diss., Berlin, 1910), pp. 86 ff.

58. Becker, p. 87, states that Weise faithfully adopted Gracián's teachings: a political man is he who, because of his character, can simultaneously please others and be prosperous himself.

59. Vol. XXVIII (Leipzig and Halle: Johann Heinrich Zedler, 1741), col. 1528.

60. Becker, pp. 55 f.

61. Concerning Grimmelshausen's relation to Weise, see Hirsch, *Bürgertum,* pp. 45 f.

62. (Bl. A 2 b ff.), as quoted by Hirsch, *Bürgertum,* p. 72.

63. Concerning Riemer, comp. Hirsch, *Bürgertum,* pp. 60 ff.

64. Hirsch, *Bürgertum,* p. 70; also comp. Becker, pp. 51 f.

Chapter Three

1. See Walther Ernst Schäfer, "Hinweg nun Amadis und deinesgleichen Grillen," *GRM,* N.F. XV (1965), 366-84.

2. Regarding Zesen's translations see p. 25.

3. Müller, p. 16.

4. An excellent comparison of the two genres is contained in Richard Alewyn's essay "Der Roman des Barock."

5. Johann Christoph Männling (1658-1723), *Arminius enucleatus* (1708) and *Lohensteinius sententiosus* (1710).

6. Heliodor's *Ethiopian Stories* had been translated into German by Johann Tschorn in 1559 and published in seven editions by 1624.

7. See Friedrich Stöffler, *Die Romane des Andreas Heinrich Buchholtz (1607-71)* (Diss. Marburg, 1918) and Cholevius, pp. 117-51.

8. Cf. Blake Lee Spahr, *Anton Ulrich and Aramena. The Genesis and Development of a Baroque Novel.* University of California Publications in Modern Philology, Vol. 76 (Berkeley and Los Angeles: University of California Press, 1966).

9. See Spahr, *Anton Ulrich,* p. 159.

10. Additional identifications in Spahr, *Anton Ulrich,* p. 153.

11. See Herbert Singer, "Die Prinzessin von Ahlden: Verwandlungen einer höfischen Sensation in der Literatur des 18. Jahrhunderts," *Euphorion,* IL (1955), 305-34.

12. Comp. Clemens Lugowski, "Die märchenhafte Enträtselung der Wirklichkeit im heroisch-galanten Roman," in: Richard Alewyn (ed.), *Deutsche Barockforschung* (Cologne, Berlin: Kiepenheuer & Witsch, 2nd. ed., 1966), p. 373.

13. Reinhard Fink, "Die Staatsromane des Herzogs Anton Ulrich von Braunschweig," *Zeitschrift für deutsche Geisteswissenschaft,* IV (1941), 58.

14. See Wolfgang Bender, *Verwirrung und Entwirrung in der "Octavia / Roemische Geschichte" Herzog Anton Ulrichs von Braunschweig* (Diss., Cologne, 1964), p. 88.

15. *Ibid.,* p. 13.

16. Concerning the following, see Blake Lee Spahr, "Der Barockroman als Wirklichkeit und Illusion," in: *Deutsche Romantheorien,* ed. Reinhold Grimm (Frankfurt a.M., Bonn: Athenäum, 1968), pp. 17-28.

17. See Spahr, "Der Barockroman," p. 25, and *idem,* "Protean Stability in the Baroque Novel," *GR,* XL (1965), 256 ff.

18. See Cholevius, pp. 213 f.

19. See *ibid.,* pp. 232 f.

20. Fink, p. 55.

21. *Goethes Werke,* Hamburger Ausgabe, Vol. 7 (Hamburg: Christian Wegner, 4th. ed., 1959), p. 360.

22. Alewyn, "Der Roman des Barock," p. 21.

23. See Luise Laporte, *Lohensteins "Arminius": Ein Dokument des deutschen Literaturbarock.* Germanische Studien, Vol. 48 (Berlin: Emil Ebering, 1927), pp. 5 ff., and Max Wehrli, *Das barocke Geschichtsbild in Lohensteins Arminius.* Wege zur Dichtung, Vol. 31 (Frauenfeld, Leipzig: Huber & Co., 1938). Cholevius, pp. 377 ff., had already pointed out the patriotic tendency of the novel.

24. Laporte, p. 11.

25. *Ibid.,* p. 76.

26. See Elida Maria Szarota, *Lohensteins Arminius als Zeitroman: Sichtweisen des Spätbarock* (Bern and Munich: Francke, 1970).

27. See Edward Verhofstadt, *Daniel Casper von Lohenstein: Untergehende Wertwelt und ästhetischer Illusionismus* (Bruges: De Tempel, 1964), p. 104.

28. See Wehrli, p. 90.

29. Concerning the literary influence of *Die Asiatische Banise,* see Wolfgang Pfeiffer-Belli, *Die asiatische Banise: Studien zur Geschichte des höfisch-historischen Romans in Deutschland.* Germanische Studien, Vol. 220 (Berlin: Emil Ebering, 1940), pp. 157 ff.

30. Johann Georg Hamann, *Fortsetzung der Asiatischen Banise, Oder des bluthigen und muthigen Pegu,* Zweyter Theil (Leipzig, 1724).

31. Christian Ernst Fidelius (pseud.), *Die Englische Banise Oder Begebenheiten der Printzessin von Sussex* (Frankfurt und Leipzig, 1754).

32. Francisci probably knew this work in a French translation: *Les voyages avantureux De Fernand Mendez Pinto,* Fidellement Traduit par Portugais en Francois par le Sieur Bernard Figuier Gentilhomme Portugais [...] (Paris, 1645).

33. See note 28.

34. See Wolfgang Pfeiffer-Belli, p. 60.

35. Concerning Zigler's style, see Pfeiffer-Belli, pp. 106 ff., and Erika Schön, *Der Stil von Ziegler's "Asiatischer Banise"* (Diss., Greifswald, 1933).

36. See Pfeiffer-Belli, p. 126.

37. The original *libretto* was written by Nicolò Beregan; and the opera was first performed in 1671 in Venice.

38. See Herbert Singer, "Joseph in Ägypten: Zur Erzählkunst des 17. und 18. Jahrhunderts," *Euphorion,* XLVIII (1954), 257.

39. Concerning Grimmelshausen's sources, see M. J. Deuschle, *Die Verarbeitung Biblischer Stoffe im deutschen Roman des Barock* (Amsterdam: H. J. Paris, 1927), pp. 41 ff.

40. Advertisement in the catalogue for the fall book fair in Leipzig, 1666.

41. See Clara Stucki, *Grimmelshausens und Zesens Josephsromane: Ein Vergleich zweier Barockdichter.* Wege zur Dichtung, Vol. 15 (Leipzig: Münster-Presse, 1933), p. 35.

42. Proximus and Dietwald are also socially humiliated, before they are raised to their former splendor and greatness.

43. See Stucki, p. 57.

44. In both cases, the adjective *teutsch* is used for "honest, upright," as Grimmelshausen uses it several times.

45. Volker Meid, Nachwort to *A,* p. 18°. Concerning Zesen's sources, also see Willi Beyersdorff, *Studien zu Philipp von Zesens biblischen Romanen "Assenat" und "Simson."* Form und Geist, Vol. 11 (Leipzig: Hermann Eichblatt), pp. 11 ff.

46. Körnchen, p. 117, judges *Assenat* negatively because of these cumbersome notes.

47. Zesen has used Grimmelshausen's Joseph novel as a source,

but he rejects his predecessor's simple style. In his notes he especially criticizes Grimmelshausen's lack of scholarly basis, which in turn prompted Grimmelshausen to carry on the controversy against Zesen's *Assenat* in *WV* I. Concerning this literary feud, see Stucki, pp. 131 ff. and Deuschle, pp. 51 ff.

48. Concerning the essayistic insertions, see Volker Meid, *Zesens Romankunst* (Diss., Frankfurt a.M., 1966), pp. 50 f., upon which this author has based his remarks.

49. Stucki, p. 110.

50. See Meid, *Zesens Romankunst*, pp. 46 f.

51. Stucki, pp. 129 f.

52. Obviously, these reasons are very superficial. It appears hardly justifiable to classify *Assenat* as a courtly saints' legend, as Herbert Singer does in "Joseph in Ägypten," 253 ff. See Meid's criticism in Meid, *Zesens Romankunst*, pp. 73 ff.

53. See Meid, *Zesens Romankunst*, pp. 60 ff.

54. Concerning the style of *Assenat*, see the more detailed analyses by Stucki, pp. 114 ff., and Meid, *Zesens Romankunst*, pp. 80 ff. See also Beyersdorff, pp. 73 ff.

55. Meid, *Zesens Romankunst*, p. 97.

56. Concerning the use of onomatopoeia and hyperbole, not treated here, see Meid, *Zesens Romankunst*, pp. 99 f. and Stucki, pp. 120 f.

57. *Der Durchlauchtigsten Hebreerinnen* JISKA REBEKKA RAHEL ASSENATH *und* SEERA *Helden=Geschichte* (Leipzig and Luneburg, 1697). Concerning Meier, see Singer, "Joseph in Ägypten," 264 ff.

58. See Benjamin Wedel, *Geheime Nachrichten und Briefe von Herrn* MENANTES *Leben und Schrifften* (Cologne, 1731). See also H. Vogel, *Christian Friedrich Hunold (Menantes) (1681-1721): Sein Leben und seine Werke* (Leipzig: Emil Gräfe, 1897), pp. 7 f. and Hans Wagener, *Die Komposition der Romane Christian Friedrich Hunolds*. University of California Publications in Modern Philology, Vol. 94 (Berkeley and Los Angeles: University of California Press, 1969), pp. 9 ff.

59. In older scholarly literature, Bohse is often called the founder of the gallant novel. Since Hunold is considered today the more important writer, Bohse's novels are not treated here.

60. Herbert Singer, *Der deutsche Roman zwischen Barock und Rokoko*. Literatur und Leben, N.F. Vol. 6 (Cologne, Graz: Böhlau, 1963); see also Singer, *Der galante Roman*.

61. Her daughter, Sophie Dorothea (1666-1726) married Georg Ludwig, the crown prince of Hanover, who became king of England (George I).

62. Singer, *Der galante Roman*, pp. 50 ff.

63. *Ibid.*, p. 52.

64. Reprint, ed. Hans Mayer (Munich: Rogner & Bernhard, 1968).

65. Reprint in: *Vorboten der bürgerlichen Kultur,* ed. Friedrich Brüggemann. DLE, Reihe Aufklärung, Vol. 4 (Leipzig, 1931; photomechanical reprint: Darmstadt: Wissenschaftliche Buchgesellschaft, 1964).

Chapter Four

1. Singer, *Der galante Roman,* p. 24.

2. Just like "Robinson," names such as "Simplicissimus" and "Banise" were misused by advertisement. *Simplicissimus redivivus* (1743), for example, contains war reports, anti-French polemics, and cooking recipes.

3. See Marianne Spiegel, *Der Roman und sein Publikum im früheren 18. Jahrhundert (1700-1767).* Abhandlungen zur Kunst-, Musik- und Literaturwissenschaft, Vol. 41 (Bonn: H. Bouvier, 1967).

Selected Bibliography

PRIMARY SOURCES

(ANONYMOUS). *Amadis. Erstes Buch*, ed. Adelbert von Keller. Reprint of the edition Stuttgart, 1857 (= Bibliothek des Literarischen Vereins in Stuttgart, Vol. XL). Darmstadt: Wissenschaftliche Buchgesellschaft, 1963.

(ANONYMOUS). *Leben vnd Wandel Lazaril von Tormes: Vnd beschreibung, Waß derselbe fur vnglück vnd widerwertigkeitt außgestanden hat.* Verdeutzscht (Breslau) 1614, ed. Hermann Tiemann. Glückstadt: Maximilian-Gesellschaft in Hamburg, 1951. (= *LT*)

BEER, JOHANN. *Das Narrenspital sowie Jucundi Jucundissimi Wunderliche Lebens-Beschreibung*, ed. Richard Alewyn, Rowohlts Klassiker, Vol. 9. Hamburg: Rowohlt, 1957. (= *JJ*)

————. *Kurtzweilige Sommer=Täge*. Abdruck der einzigen Ausgabe (1683), ed. Wolfgang Schmitt, Neudrucke deutscher Literaturwerke des XVI. und XVII. Jahrhunderts, Vol. 324. Halle a.S.: VEB Max Niemeyer, 1958. (= *KS*)

————. *Die teutschen Winter=Nächte & Die kurzweiligen Sommer-Täge*, ed. Richard Alewyn. Frankfurt a.M.: Insel, 1963.

GRIMMELSHAUSEN, HANS JACOB CHRISTOFFEL VON. *Der Abentheurliche Simplicissimus Teutsch und Continuatio des abentheurlichen Simplicissimi*, ed. Rolf Tarot. Grimmelshausen, Gesammelte Werke in Einzelausgaben. Unter Mitarbeit von Wolfgang Bender und Franz Günter Sieveke hrsg. v. Rolf Tarot. Tübingen: Max Niemeyer, 1967. (= *ST*)

————. *Des Vortrefflich Keuschen Josephs in Egypten Lebensbeschreibung samt des Musai Lebens-Lauff*, ed. Wolfgang Bender. Grimmelshausen, Gesammelte Werke in Einzelausgaben. Tübingen, Max Niemeyer, 1968. (= *KJ*)

HUNOLD, CHRISTIAN FRIEDRICH (pseud. MENANTES). *Die liebenswürdige Adalie*. Faksimiledruck nach der Ausgabe von 1702, with an interpretive essay by Herbert Singer. Deutsche Neudrucke, Reihe Texte des 18. Jahrhunderts. Stuttgart: J. B. Metzlersche Verlagsbuchhandlung, 1967.

KACZEROWSKY, KLAUS (ed.). *Schäferromane des Barock*, Rowohlts Klassiker, Vol. 530/31 (Texte deutscher Literatur 1500-1800). Hamburg, Rowohlt, 1970. (= *AA*)

173

OPITZ, MARTIN. *Schäfferey von der Nimfen Hercinie,* ed. Peter Rusterholz. Reclams Universal-Bibliothek, Vol. 8594. Stuttgart: Philipp Reclam jun., 1969.

REUTER, CHRISTIAN. *Schelmuffsky.* Abdruck der vollständigen Ausgabe 1696. 1697, ed. A. Schullerus. Neudrucke deutscher Literaturwerke des XVI. und XVII. Jahrhunderts, Vol. 57/58. Halle a.S.: Max Niemeyer, 1885. (= S)

THOMAS, JOHANN. *Damon und Lysille. 1663 und 1665,* with an interpretive essay by Herbert Singer. Hamburg: Maximilian-Gesellschaft, 1966. (= DL)

WEISE, CHRISTIAN. *Die drei ärgsten Erznarren in der ganzen Welt.* Abdruck der Ausgabe von 1673, ed. W. Braune. Neudrucke deutscher Literaturwerke des XVI. und XVII. Jahrhunderts, Vol. 12-14. Halle a.S.: Max Niemeyer, 1878. (= E)

ZESEN, PHILIPP VON. *Assenat. 1670,* ed. Volker Meid. Deutsche Neudrucke, Reihe Barock, Bd. 9. Tübingen: Max Niemeyer, 1967. (= A)

—————. *Ritterholds von Blauen Adriatische Rosemund. Amsterdam 1645,* ed. Max Hermann Jellinek. Neudrucke deutscher Literaturwerke des XVI. und XVII. Jahrhunderts, Vol. 160-63. (= AR)

ZIGLER UND KLIPHAUSEN, HEINRICH ANSHELM VON. *Asiatische Banise.* Vollständiger Text nach der Ausgabe von 1707 unter Berücksichtigung des Erstdrucks von 1689, with an interpretive essay by Wolfgang Pfeiffer-Belli. Darmstadt: Wissenschaftliche Buchgesellschaft, 1966. (= AB)

SECONDARY SOURCES

ALEWYN, RICHARD. *Johann Beer. Studien zum Roman des 17. Jahrhunderts.* Palaestra, Vol. 181. Leipzig: Mayer und Müller, 1932. The first comprehensive study of Johann Beer's novels, documenting the rediscovery of the author. Alewyn contrasts Beer as a "realist" to Grimmelshausen as a "naturalist."

—————. "Der Roman des Barock," in: Hans Steffen (ed.), *Formkräfte der deutschen Dichtung vom Barock bis zur Gegenwart.* Göttingen: Vandenhoeck & Ruprecht, 2nd. ed. 1967, pp. 21-34. A comparison of the picaresque and the courtly-historical novel according to subject, structure, and underlying world view. The pastoral novel is not included in the discussion.

BECHTOLD, ARTUR. "Schelmenroman," in: Merker, Paul und Wolfgang Stammler (eds.), *Reallexikon der deutschen Literaturgeschichte,* Vol. III. Berlin: Walter de Gruyter, 1928/29, 164-67. A short summary of the introduction of the Spanish picaresque novel in Germany and a brief characterization of the main examples.

BOBERTAG, FELIX. *Geschichte des Romans und der ihm verwandten Dichtungsgattungen in Deutschland.* 2 vols. Breslau: A. Gosohorsky, 1876/84. The most important of the earlier histories of the German novel, which has hardly been surpassed with regard to detailed factual information, but is nevertheless outdated in its critical judgments.

BORCHERDT, HANS HEINRICH. *Geschichte des Romans und der Novelle in Deutschland. I Teil: Vom frühen Mittelalter bis zu Wieland.* Leipzig: Weber, 1926. The second volume of this work never appeared. Although the author is more interested in *Geistesgeschichte* (history of ideas), often not sufficiently focusing on individual works, this is one of the few competent histories of the older German novel.

CHOLEVIUS, LEO. *Die bedeutendsten deutschen Romane des siebzehnten Jahrhunderts. Ein Beitrag zur Geschichte der deutschen Literatur.* Reprint of the edition Leipzig 1866: Darmstadt: Wissenschaftliche Buchgesellschaft, 1965. The appearance of this reprint, almost one hundred years after its first publication, is sufficient proof of the value of this work. Although some of the author's analyses have become outdated in the meantime, Cholevius' work is rich in ideas. Of especial value are his detailed plot summaries of the most important German Baroque novels.

COHN, EGON. *Gesellschaftsideale und Gesellschaftsroman des 17. Jahrhunderts. Studien zur deutschen Bildungsgeschichte.* Germanische Studien, Vol. 13. Berlin: E. Ebering, 1921. In this stimulating monograph, Cohn attempts to characterize the intellectual atmosphere of the seventeenth century and the development of the German novel, its origins, foreign models, and the innovative achievements of the most outstanding German writers of that period.

FLEMMING, WILLI. "Heroisch-galanter Roman," in: *Reallexikon der deutschen Literaturgeschichte*, 2nd. edition, ed. Werner Kohlschmidt and Wolfgang Mohr. Vol. I. Berlin: Walter de Gruyter, 1958, 647-50. A short summary of genre criteria and the history of the courtly-historical novel with an excellent bibliography.

HEIDENREICH, HELMUT (ed.). *Pikarische Welt. Schriften zum Europäischen Schelmenroman.* Wege der Forschung, Vol. 163. Darmstadt: Wissenschaftliche Buchgesellschaft, 1969. A collection of the most important scholarly essays and book excerpts dealing with the European picaresque novel, exemplifying the characteristics of the Spanish models and the variation of the genre among the national literatures of Europe.

HIRSCH, ARNOLD. *Bürgertum und Barock im deutschen Roman.* 2nd. edition, ed. Herbert Singer. Literatur und Leben, N.F. Vol. 1.

Köln/Graz: Böhlau, 1957. This monograph, which demonstrates the author's familiarity with a very broad range of rare seventeenth-century novels, deals with the intrusion of bourgeois elements into the German Baroque novel during the final decades of the seventeenth century.

—————. "Barockroman und Aufklärungsroman," *Etudes Germaniques,* IX (1954), 97-111. A study which traces the development of the German Baroque novel and contrasts it with the novels of the Enlightenment.

KNIGHT, K. G. *Deutsche Romane der Barockzeit. Auszüge aus dem erzählenden Schrifttum des siebzehnten Jahrhunderts.* London: Methuen & Co., Ltd., 1969. As indicated by the subtitle, this is an edition of excerpts from seventeenth-century narrative prose. Of interest is the introductory essay by the editor, which describes, in a general fashion, the origin and various types of the German Baroque novel.

LUGOWSKI, CLEMENS. *Wirklichkeit und Dichtung. Untersuchungen zur Wirklichkeitsauffassung Heinrich von Kleists.* Frankfurt a.M.: Moritz Diesterweg, 1936. Chap. I: "Die märchenhafte Enträtselung der Wirklichkeit im heroisch-galaten Roman." Reprinted in: Richard Alewyn (ed.), *Deutsche Barockforschung. Dokumentation einer Epoche.* Neue Wissenschaftliche Bibliothek, Vol. 7. Köln/Berlin: Kiepenheuer & Witsch, 2nd. edition, 1966, 372-91. The author points out the purposely established scheme of confusion characteristic of the courtly-historical novel, using as an example Duke Anton Ulrich's *Aramena.*

MEYER, HEINRICH. *Der deutsche Schäferroman des 17. Jahrhunderts.* Diss. Freiburg i. Br., 1927; published: Dorpat 1928. Definition, classification and history of the German pastoral novel, including detailed plot summaries and short analyses of the individual works.

—————. "Schäferroman," in: Merker, Paul and Wolfgang Stammler (eds.), *Reallexikon der deutschen Literaturgeschichte,* Vol. III. Berlin: Walter de Gruyter, 1928/29, 151-54. A short summary of the author's above mentioned dissertation, which is limited to classification and a short sketch of the development of the German pastoral novel.

MÜLLER, GÜNTHER. "Barockromane und Barockroman," in: *Literaturwissenschaftliches Jahrbuch der Görres-Gesellschaft.* Vol. IV (1929): "Barock." Freiburg i. Br.: Herder, 1-29. The first comprehensive essay on the various subgenres or types of the German Baroque novel, which, in spite of the author's emphasis on *Geistesgeschichte,* offers a great deal of factual information and portrays the development of the genre as culminating in Duke Anton Ulrich's novels.

SINGER, HERBERT. *Der deutsche Roman zwischen Barock und Rokoko.* Literatur und Leben, N.F., Vol. 6. Köln/Graz: Böhlau, 1963. A comprehensive description of the gallant novel, including a comprehensive bibliography of original editions. Singer focuses on Christian Friedrich Hunold, whose *Liebenswürdige Adalie* he utilizes for the purpose of pointing out the new and unique features of the gallant as compared to the courtly-historical novel.

——————. *Der galante Roman.* Sammlung Metzler, Vol. 10. Stuttgart: Metzler, 1961. A shortened, introductory version of the above book.

SPAHR, BLAKE LEE. "Protean Stability in the Baroque Novel," *GR* (1965), 253-60. Using Duke Anton Ulrich's *Aramena* as a model, Spahr describes the confounding of reality and illusion, *Schein und Sein,* in the heroes of the German Baroque novel.

——————. "Der Barockroman als Wirklichkeit und Illusion," in: *Deutsche Romantheorien,* ed. Reinhold Grimm. Frankfurt a.M./ Bonn: Athenäum, 1968, pp. 17-28. An attempt to characterize the German Baroque novel as such, using Duke Anton Ulrich's *Aramena* as an example. Thus, Spahr limits himself to the courtly-historical novel.

STERN, GERHARD WILHELM. *Die Liebe im Roman des 17. Jahrhunderts.* Germanische Studien, Vol. 120. Berlin: Ebering, 1932. A study tracing the concept and the description of love in all three genres of the German Baroque novel.

THURNHER, EUGEN. "Das Formgesetz des barocken Romans," *Innsbrucker Beiträge zur Kulturwissenschaft,* Vol. 6. Germanistische Abhandlungen, ed. Karl Kurt Klein and Eugen Thurnher. Innsbruck: Sprachwissenschaftliches Institut der Universität Innsbruck, 1959. A brief general characterization of the German Baroque novel, lacking a clear discrimination between the various subgenres.

WEYDT, GÜNTHER. "Der deutsche Roman von der Renaissance und Reformation bis zu Goethes Tod," in: *Deutsche Philologie im Aufriß,* ed. Wolfgang Stammler, Vol. 2. Berlin and Bielefeld: Erich Schmidt, 1960, cols. 1217-1356. A concise history of the early German novel, which, in the section covering the Baroque, is subdivided into the three genres discussed here.

Index